the Cook's Book of Ponder

Fathoming 18TH century cooking

English Edition

Ex Coquu

the Cook's Book of Ponder
Fathoming 18TH Century Cooking
English Edition

Copyright © 2022

All rights reserved. No part of this publication may be reproduced, distributed, or transmitted in any form or by any means, including electronic or mechanical methods, without prior written permission of the author, except in the case of brief quotations embodied in critical reviews and certain other noncommercial uses permitted by copyright law or where contents are public domain.

Paperback ISBN: 979-8-8229-0181-0
eBook ISBN: 979-8-8229-0182-7

Table of Contents

Preface i
Weights and Measures iv
Cooking Methods vii
Terminology viii
Interpretation of Bullets ix
Time and Temperature x
Stocks and Sauces 1
   Ketchup. 1
      Fish Sauce 2
      Soy Sauce 5
      Worcestershire Sauce 7
   Stocks 8
      Brown Stock 8
      Veal Stock 10
      Chicken Stock 12
      Fish Stock 12
      Fish Stock 12
      Vegetable Stock 14
   Sauces 17
      Espagnole 18
      Mushroom Sauce 20
      Allemande Sauce 21
      Mushroom Sauce I 22
      Mushroom Sauce II 22
      Sauce Robert 22
      Béchamel 23
      18TH Century Béchamel 24
      Béchamel 25
      Mornay 25
      Velouté 26

Suprême	26
Charcutière	26
Soubise	27
Anchovy Sauce	28
Hollandaise Sauce	29
Fruits and Salads	**32**
Baked Apples	32
Stewed Apples	32
Fried Apples	34
Applesauce	34
Apple Butter	34
Poached Pears	35
Stewed Pears	36
Basic Salad	37
Basic Salad Oil	37
Other Basic Salad	38
Soups and Broth	**40**
Beef Soup	40
Bisque	41
Clear Soup	43
Cream Soup	43
Bisque	43
White Bean Soup	43
White Chicken Soup	43
Mushroom Soup	44
Shrimp Bisque	44
Pea Soup	44
Cream of Onion Soup	46
Egg Soup	47
Beef	**49**
Corned Beef	49
Pastrami	50

- Country Fried Steak ... 50
- Veal Francaise ... 53
- German Jägerschnitzel ... 53
- Scaloppinedi Vitello al Marsala ... 53
- Roast Beef ... 53
- Grilled Steak ... 55

Chicken ... 57
- Chicken in Mushroom Sauce ... 57
- Fried Chicken ... 58
- Chicken in White Wine & Cream ... 60
- Barbecue Chicken ... 62
- Chicken Fricassee ... 63

Pork ... 65
- Pork Chops Robert ... 65
- Cumberland Sausage ... 66
- Cured Ham ... 67

Fish ... 70
- Salmon ... 70
- Fried Carp ... 72
- Southern Fried Catfish ... 73
- Fish and Chips ... 73
- Tartar Sauce ... 74
- Poached Flounder ... 74

Turkey ... 76
- Bread Stuffing ... 76

Vegetables ... 78
- Cabbage ... 78
- Spinach ... 79
- Creamed Spinach ... 80
- Carrots ... 81
- Candied Carrots ... 81
- Fried Cauliflower ... 82

- Broccoli 82
- Peas 83
- Pastas and Potatoes 85
  - Vermicelli 85
  - Pasta Dough 86
  - Vermicelli 86
  - Maccheroncini 87
  - Macaroni & Cheese 87
  - Candied Sweet Potatoes 88
  - Sweet Potato Pie 89
  - Boiled Potatoes 90
  - Grilled Potatoes 90
  - Fried Potatoes 91
  - Country Style Potatoes 92
  - Twice Baked Potatoes 92
  - Scalloped Potatoes 94
  - Au Gratin Potatoes 94
- Beans and Rice 96
  - Ham and Beans 96
  - Red Beans 97
  - Red Beans and Rice 98
  - Refried Beans 99
  - Baked Beans 101
  - French Cut Green Beans 103
- Eggs, Butter and Cheese 105
  - Omelet 105
  - Deviled Eggs 106
  - Quiche 109
  - Cream Cheese 112
  - Cheddar, Cheshire, Gloucester 114
  - Roquefort 115
  - Parmigiano-Reggiano 116

Brie 117
Butter 118
Crème Fraîche 118
Bread 119
White Bread 119
Dinner Roll 123
English Muffin 123
Savoiardi 123
French Biscuits 124
Pastry Dough 126
Pie Dough 126
Puff Pastry 127
Puddings and Syllabubs 130
Bread Pudding 130
Rice Pudding 131
Rice Pudding 131
English Almond Custard 133
Apple Dumpling 135
English Apple tart 136
English Orange Tart 137
English Lemon Tart 138
Syllabub 144
Pies 145
Apple Pie I 145
Apple Pie II 146
Pumpkin Pie 148
Chicken Pot Pie 150
Mincemeat Pie 151
Cakes and Cookies 153
Trifle 153
Crepes 154
English Caraway Cake 155

    Gingerbread Cookie 156
    Lemon Chiffon Cake 158
    New York Cheesecake 159
    Raisin Butter Cake 161
    Cornbread 162
    Corn Pudding 163
    Queens Cake aka modern Gingerbread Cake. 164
    Cake Icing 165
    Macaroons 166
    Sugar Cookie 167
    Gingerbread 168
Tarts and Puffs 169
    Pizzelles 169
    Meringue Cookie 170
    Lemon Meringue Cookie 171
    Apple Tart 172
    Lemon or Orange Tart 172
Custards and Creams 175
    English Pudding 175
    English Orange Pudding 176
    Crème Brûlée 177
    Custard 178
    Whipped Cream 179
    Apricot Ice-Cream 180
    Lemon Ice-Cream 181
    Orange Ice-Cream 181
    Chocolate Ice-Cream 182
Fritters 184
    Basic Fritter 184
    Apple Fritter 184
    Fritter Batter 185
    Cheese Fritter 186

Pickling and Preserves 188
    White Vinegar 188
    Sauerkraut 189
    Sweet Pickles 190
    Pickled Cucumbers 191
    Pickled Mushrooms 193
    Strawberry Preserves 194
    Peach Preserves 195

Jams, Jellies and Marmalades 196
    Apricot Jam 196
    Strawberry Jam 197
    Jell-O® 198
    Orange Marmalade 199
    Apricot Marmalade 199

Candies 201
    Raspberry Candy 201
    French Praline 202
    Candied Peels 203

Wines 205
    Blackberry Wine 205
    Cherry Wine 206
    Orange Wine 206
    White or Red Wine 207
    Fortified Wine 210

Ciders, Beer and Ale 211
    Cider 211
    Spruce Beer 212
    Leavening 213

Cordials and Waters 215
    Lemon Brandy 215
    Orange Brandy 215

Raspberry Brandy 216
　　Mint Water 217
　　Rose Water 218
　　Orange Water 219
Sources 220

Preface

My passion - cooking.

My interest - history.

So where did it all begin?

This is my culinary adventure to understand the historical values and cooking techniques from the 18TH century.

My goal is to interpret the recipes and recreate the cooking process using the same techniques in a modern kitchen.

" FOR TO MAKE GRONDEN BENES. I.

Take benes and dry hem in a nost or in an Ovene and hulle hem wele and wyndewe out þe hulk and wayshe hem clene an do hem to seeþ in gode broth an ete hem with Bacon.

Seriously, I wonder how much wine the individual consumed before writing down this recipe. I envision an old cook sitting at a table, with a partially consumed gallon of wine, trying to explain to his apprentice how to cook while the apprentice is writing down the recipe exactly how he hears it.

Take and dry beans in an oven. Remove the bean [seeds] from the hull and clean them. Place the beans in a pot of good broth with bacon and simmer until the beans are soft.

This recipe is a basic ham and bean soup lacking in flavor from seasonings. Generally, ham was salt cured and smoked to preserve the meat for later use. Salt and smoke are the two main flavors in the dish.

TART DE BRY. XX.VIII. VI.

Take a Crust ynche depe in a trape. take zolkes of Ayren rawe & chese ruayn. & medle it & þe zolkes togyder. and do þerto powdour gyngur. sugur. safroun. and salt. do it in a trape, bake it and serue it forth. de Bry.

Everyone loves a good tart; however, trying to interpret this recipe is definitely a challenge.

Put pie dough in a one-inch-deep pan. Combine yolks and cheese in a bowl with powdered ginger, sugar, saffron, and salt thoroughly mixing. Spoon the filling onto the pie dough and bake until the crust is golden brown and the filling is set. The recipe is similar to the modern-day cheesecake.

While some argue the cheese in the recipe is the modern-day Brie, others believe it is cheese from the region of Brie located in France.

Weights and Measures

Traditional names like foot, pound, and gallon were used throughout the British Empire; however, each foot, pound, or gallon varied from region to region. During the 14TH century the Winchester Standard was introduced to create uniformity between trading goods, for example, the yard. The yard was three feet in length. Each foot was divided into 12 inches, and each inch had a length of three barleycorns. Establishing standard units of measurement allowed consistent measuring of distance, volume, and weight. One example of measuring volume and weight was the establishment of the wine gallon measuring 231 cubic inches and weighing eight pounds.

The English doubling system, or double standard, was also known as avoirdupois standard and was instituted in the 16TH century where measurements were doubled from the prior.

By the 18TH century there were three common standards:

- Troy, t – weighing precious metals and stones at 12 ounces per pound,
- Avoirdupois – weighing other dry goods at 16 ounces per pound,
- Apothecaries, ap – weighing medicines at 12 ounces per pound.

Weights and Measures Table

Unit	Abbreviation	Weight
Peck		16 pounds
Gallon		8 pounds
Pottle		4 pounds
Quart		2 pounds
Pint		16 ounces
Pound	t	16 ounces 240 pennyweight
Pound	ap	12 ounces
Cup		8 ounces
Gill		5 ounces
Tea Cup		4 ounces
Ounce		2 tablespoons

Weights and Measures Table

Unit	Abbreviation	Weight
Ounce	t	20 pennyweight
Ounce	ap	8 drachms
Tablespoon		1/2 ounce
Teaspoon		.167 ounce 1/3 tablespoon
Teaspoon	prior to the 16TH century	.125 ounce 1/4 tablespoon
Pennyweight	t	4 drachms 1/2 ounce
Drachm	ap	3 scruples .0125 ounce
Scruple	ap	1/3 drachm
Grain		.002083 ounce
Grain	t	.042 pennyweight
Grain	ap	.0166 drachm .05 scruple

Cooking Methods

Dry heat method:

- Cooking without a liquid such as hot air, hot metal [pan or pot], or hot fat.
  - ✓ Open fire,
  - ✓ Open hearth fireplace,
    - Fireplaces heat by radiation. Objects [bricks] are heated by flames or coals. Once the bricks are hot, heat is radiated out cooking the food within the fireplace area.
  - ✓ Cast iron range,
  - ✓ Brick range with a perforated cast-iron top,
  - ✓ Brick or cast-iron oven.

Moist heat method:

- Cooking using a liquid such as stock, sauce or steam.

Terminology

Broth	Liquid in which meat or vegetables are cooked.
Gravy	A well-seasoned broth.
Stock	Gravy.
Sauce	Stock thickened with a roux (equal portions of flour and fat).
Mum	Ale.
Allegar	Vinegar.
Sack-Fortified wine	Marsala, Vermouth, Sherry, Port wine.
Sugar	Brown sugar.
Refined sugar	White sugar.
Double refined sugar	Powdered sugar.
Blade	One pass across a grater.
Rusk	Stale bread.
Sachet	Spices contained in a cheesecloth bag containing black peppercorns, garlic clove, bay leaf, and whole cloves.
Bouquet garni	Herbs tied in a bundle containing parsley and thyme stems, leek, and celery leaf.
Mirepoix	50% onion, 25% each of celery and carrot diced medium.

Interpretation of Bullets

18TH century recipe ingredients.

❖ *18TH century interpretation of recipe.*

- Food history.

➢ **Recipe**: Modern procedure created from the interpretation of the 18TH century recipe.

Note:

RECIPE – Highlighted wording in recipes are recipes provided in this book.

Time and Temperature

Time and Temperature Table

Temperature	Degree in Fahrenheit	Hand over heat source in seconds
Low Softly	250-300	8 to 9
Medium-Low Slow	301-350	6 to 7
Medium, Flack, Gently, or Moderate	301-350	4 to 5
Medium-High Quick	351-400	2 to 3
High	401-500	2 seconds or less

To determine the temperature of the heat, using the back of your hand, place it over the heat source using the above chart.

Stocks and Sauces

18TH century cookbooks reference the following words in cooking:

- **Gravy**-a well-seasoned broth,
- **Sauce**-a thickened stock so fat does not rise to the surface, and
- **Stock**-carrying the same meaning as gravy.

The word Gravy is from Anglo-French referring to a seasoned broth from cooked meat and not by today's meaning of a thickened sauce.

During the 17TH century, we see the beginning of transformation to modern day cooking by François-Pierre de La Varenne, and the continuation of refining the cooking method in the 18TH century by Marie-Antoine Carême; however, it was Georges-Auguste Escoffier in the 19TH century that standardized the recipes for stocks and sauces.

Ketchup.

Today's ketchup [with various spellings: catchup, catsup] is tomato based and did not appear until about a century after other types. Early ketchup started out as a general term for sauce that was made from fermented fish or soybeans brined in salt water dating back to as early as AD 535. It was not uncommon to find ketchup being made in individual households where various ingredients were being used in an attempt to recreate ketchup. They included the use of walnuts and mushrooms where, in Germany, a variety of soy sauces [ketchup] are manufactured using mushrooms. Early production of England's Worcestershire sauce used ketchup as a main ingredient. Depending on the region and trade from Asia, you would have ended up with different types or flavors of ketchup. We know the following recipes are 18TH century attempts to replicate these foreign sauces since they reference a foreign catchup.

To make Englifh Catchup.
Fish Sauce

TAKE a wide-mouthed bottle, put therein a pint of the beft white wine vinegar, putting in ten or twelve cloves of efchalot peeled and juft bruifed; then take a quarter of a pint of the beft langoon white wine, boil it a little, and put to it twelve or fourteen anchovies wafhed and fhred, and diffolve them in the wine, and when cold, put them in the bottle; then take a quarter of a pint more of white wine, and put in it mace, ginger fliced, a few cloves, a fpoonful of whole pepper juft bruifed, and let them boil all a little; when near cold, flice in almoft a whole nutmeg, and fome lemon-peel, and like wife put in two or three fpoonfuls of horfe-radifh; then ftop it clofe, and for a week fhake it once or twice a day; then ufe it; it is good to put into fifh-fauce, or any favoury difh of meat; you may add to it the clear liquor that comes from mufhrooms.

12 anchovies, cleaned and minced
10 shallots, minced
Whole clove, as needed
Lemon peel, grated
2 cups white wine vinegar
1 cup white wine
Fresh ginger, minced
1 tablespoon horseradish
1 tablespoon whole peppercorn, cracked
Ground mace, as needed
Nutmeg, grated

- Fishermen collected fresh catch salting the fish and placing them in the hull of the ship to prevent spoilage.

Generally, canned anchovies have one-third the sodium content as salted fish; therefore, when recreating this recipe, you must use fresh fish that has been salted or the recipe will be missing one important ingredient, sodium.

The same process for making sauerkraut is used to make fish and soy sauces. The main ingredient is salted and weighted down keeping the ingredients below the water line to prevent spoilage.

Fresh fish contains about 75% water. Salting the fish will extract the moisture while the fermenting process will develop the flavor. This recipe replicates foreign ketchup or today's modern-day fish sauce.

When recreating ketchup, the following rules apply:

I. If using canned anchovies, add one tablespoon non-iodized salt to this recipe,

II. If using anchovy paste, one-half teaspoon of anchovy paste is equivalent to one anchovy.

❖ *Combine two cups of white wine vinegar with 10 ounces of minced shallots in a wide mouth bottle. Using a sauce pot, bring one-half cup of white wine to a boil. Reduce the temperature to medium and add 12 minced anchovies whisking until the anchovies have partially dissolved into the wine. Remove the pot from the heat and allow to cool to room temperature. Pour the wine into the wide mouth bottle. Clean the pot and add one-half cup of white wine, one-half teaspoon of ground mace, and three tablespoons of black peppercorns bringing to a boil. Remove from heat and allow to cool to room temperature. Pour the wine into the wide mouth bottle adding one-half teaspoon of ground nutmeg, two tablespoons of grated lemon peel, and one tablespoon of grated horseradish. Cover the jar with a lid and shake twice daily for two weeks. Strain the sauce through a coffee filter, bottle, and refrigerate.*

Another Way.

Soy Sauce

TAKE the large flaps of mufhrooms, pick nothing but the ftraws and dirt from it, then lay them in a broad earthen pan, ftrew a good deal of falt over them, let them lie till next morning, then with your hand break them, put them into a ftewpan, let them boil a minute or two, then ftrain them through a Coarfe cloth, and wring it hard. Take out all the juice, let it ftand to fettle, then pour it off clear, run it through a thick flannel bag, (fome filter it through brown paper, but that is a very tedious way) then boil it ; to a quart of the liquor put a quarter of an ounce of whole ginger, and half a quarter of an ounce of whole pepper. Boil it brifkly a quarter of an hour, then ftrain it, and when it is cold, put it into pint bottles. In each bottle put four or five blades of mace, and fix cloves, cork it tight, and it will keep two years. This gives the beft flavour of the mufhrooms to any fauce. If you put to a pint of this catchup, a pint of mum, it will tafte like foreign catchup.

Mushrooms, cleaned and stems removed
Salt, to taste
1-1/2 teaspoons ginger, minced
3/4 teaspoon whole peppercorn, cracked
5 blades Mace
6 Cloves

❖ Using a food processor, mince [pulse] 16 ounces of whole mushroom caps with two tablespoons of non-iodized salt. Put the mushrooms into a mixing bowl and weight down by covering them with a plate and then plastic wrap. Allow the plastic wrap to hang over the side of the bowl and fill with water. Allow the mushrooms to rest for 24 hours. Carefully remove the plastic wrap pouring off only the water contained in the plastic wrap. Use a clean bowl for the next step. Pour the mushrooms into a jelly bag wringing [twisting] the bag to extract all the liquid from the mushrooms into the bowl. Allow the liquid to settle and pour the top portion of the liquid into a clean sauce pot leaving any sediment in the bottom of the bowl. Using a sauce pot, combine the mushroom liquid with one and one-half teaspoons of crushed ginger [ginger paste] and three-quarter teaspoon of cracked black peppercorns bringing to a boil. Reduce the temperature to medium-low and allow to simmer for fifteen minutes. Pour the sauce through a coffee filter removing the ginger and cracked peppercorns. Return the sauce to the pot and bring back to a boil. Remove and bottle the sauce into 16-ounce canning jars. For every 16-ounce jar filled, add two teaspoons of ground mace and six whole cloves. Cover the jars with lids and allow to rest in refrigeration for two weeks. Strain the sauce through a coffee filter, bottle, and refrigerate.

❖ *For another foreign sauce:*

  ❖ *Combine* **SOY SAUCE** *in equal portions to Mum [Ale],*

Worcestershire Sauce

➢ Using a sauce pot, combine one-quarter cup each of **FISH** and **SOY SAUCE,** one tablespoon of molasses, one teaspoon each of onion powder, garlic powder, lemon juice, and one-eighth teaspoon of cayenne pepper and thoroughly whisk. Bring to a boil. Remove from heat and allow to cool to room temperature. Strain through a coffee filter. Bottle and refrigerate.

Stocks

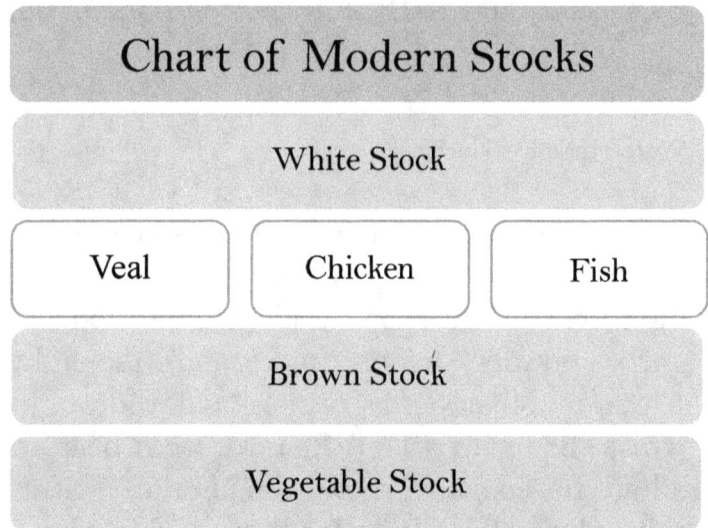

Gravy for Brown Sauces.
Brown Stock

TAKE fome Neck of Beef, cut it in thin Slices, then flour it well, and put it in a Sauce-pan, with a Slice of fat Bacon, an Onion fliced, fome Powder of fweet Marjoram, fome Pepper and Salt, cover it clofe, and put it over a flow Fire; ftir it three or four Times, and when the Gravy is brown, put fome Water to it; ftir it altogether, and let it boil about half an Hour; then ftrain it off, and take the Fat off the Top, adding a little Lemon-Juice.

1 slice bacon
1 lemon, juiced
1 neck of beef, cut into thin slices
1 onion, sliced

Salt, to taste
Marjoram, ground, as needed
Peppercorn, crushed, to taste
Water, as needed
Flour, as needed

- ❖ *Take a neck of beef or three pounds of beef and three pounds of beef bones and generously coat with bread flour. Put the beef and bones in a large stock pot with one slice of bacon, one large onion diced medium, ground marjoram, cracked black peppercorn, and salt. Cook until the beef and onions are well browned. Once browned, add enough water to cover the beef and bones. Allow to simmer for 30 minutes. Strain through a fine wire sieve. Allow to cool to room temperature and remove the fat that has risen to the top and hardened. Season with lemon juice to taste.*

The browning in the recipe comes from sautéing the flour until browned but not burnt with additional color from caramelizing [browning] the onions. As stated earlier, sauces would have been thickened with flour incorporating the fat so that it does not rise to the surface. This recipe instructs the individual to remove the fat that has risen to the surface indicating the creation of a stock and not a thickened sauce.

- ➢ For brown stock: Place four pounds of beef bones onto a roasting pan. Preheat an oven to 400°F and roast the bones until well browned. Combine the roasted bones in a large stock pot with four quarts of water. Place one-half cup of chopped onion, one-quarter cup each of chopped celery and carrots, and two tablespoons of tomato paste onto the roasting pan. Roast the ingredients, stirring occasionally, until the vegetables and tomato paste are well browned. [Tomato paste is used in place of flour for richer flavor and color]. When the vegetables and tomato paste have browned, add them to the stock pot and stir until the tomato paste has dissolved into the water. Add four stems each of parsley and thyme, one-quarter teaspoon of crushed black peppercorn, and one bay leaf to the pot. Bring to a boil. Reduce the temperature to medium-low and allow to simmer for eight hours. Skim any scum off the surface as it forms. Remove from the heat and rapidly cool. Remove any fat that has hardened on the surface and strain through a fine wire sieve. Bottle and refrigerate.

Gravy for White Sauces.

Veal Stock

TAKE Part of a Knuckle or the worft Part of a Neck of Veal, boil about a Pound of it in a Quart of Water, an Onion, fome whole Pepper, fix Cloves, a little Salt, a Bunch of fweet Herbs, half a Nutmeg fliced ; let it boil an Hour, then ftrain it off, and keep it for Ufe.

Bunch of sweet herbs
1 onion, chopped
1 pound knuckle or neck of veal
4 cups water
6 whole cloves
Salt, to taste
1/2 nutmeg, grated
Peppercorn, as needed

- ❖ *Using a large stock pot, combine one pound knuckle of veal or one-half pound of veal and one-half pound of veal bones, four cups of water, one large onion diced medium, six whole cloves, parsley and thyme stems, sage leaf, cracked black peppercorn, salt, and one-half nutmeg,`` ground. Bring to a boil. Reduce the temperature to medium-low and allow to simmer for 60 minutes. Strain through a fine wire sieve.*

- ➢ For veal stock: Using a large stock pot, combine four pounds of veal or beef bones with four quarts of water. Bring to a boil. Drain and rinse the bones. Place the bones back into the pot adding four more quarts of water, one-half cup of chopped onion, one-quarter cup each of chopped celery and carrots, four each of parsley and thyme stems, one-quarter teaspoon of crushed black peppercorn, and one bay leaf. Bring to a boil. Reduce the temperature to medium-low and allow to simmer for eight hours. Skim any scum off the top as it forms. Remove from heat and rapidly cool. Remove any fat that may have hardened on the surface and strain through a fine wire sieve. Bottle and refrigerate.

Chicken Stock

➢ Use chicken carcass instead of veal or beef bones.

Fish Stock

➢ Use fish carcass instead of veal or beef bones.

A good Stock for Fifh Soops.
Fish Stock

PREPARE Scate, Flounders, Eels, and Whiteings, lay them in a broad Gravy-pan, put in a Faggot of Thyme, Parfley and Onions, feafon them with Pepper, Salt, Cloves, and Mace; then pour in as much Water as will cover your Fifh ; put in a Head of Sellery, and fome Parfley Roots. Boil it very tender about an Hour, then ftrain it off for any Ufe, for Fifh or Meagre Pottages, This Stock will not keep above a Day. If you would make a Brown Stock you muft pafs your Fifh off in browned Butter, and ftove it, then put in your Liquor and Seafoning.

Fish, chopped
1 head of celery, chopped
1 parsley root, chopped, as necessary
Handful parsley stems

Handful thyme stems
Handful onion, chopped
Salt, to taste
Peppercorn, cracked, to taste
Clove, ground, to taste
Mace, ground, to taste
Water, as necessary

❖ *Using a large stock pot, combine four pounds of chopped fish, one head of chopped celery, one chopped parsley root, handful each of parsley, thyme, and chopped onion, salt, cracked black peppercorn, ground clove, ground mace, and enough water to cover the fish. Bring to a boil. Reduce the temperature to medium-low and allow to simmer for 60 minutes. Strain through a fine wire sieve.*

The recipe does not specify the quantity of fish to use for making the stock. It's plausible the quantity of fish to use would be equal to the weight of beef and beef bones in brown stock.

➢ For fish stock: Using a stock pot, combine four pounds fish carcass, four quarts of water, one-half cup of chopped onion, one-quarter cup each of chopped celery and carrots, four each of parsley and thyme stems, one-quarter teaspoon crushed black peppercorn, and one bay leaf. Bring to a boil. Reduce the temperature to medium-low and allow to simmer for 60 minutes. Skim any scum off top as it forms. Strain through a fine wire sieve. Bottle and refrigerate.

A Stock for an Herb-Soop.

Vegetable Stock

GET Chervil, Beets, Chards, Spinach, Sellery, Leeks, and fuch like Herbs, with two or three large Crufts of Bread, fome Butter, a Bunch of fweet Herbs, and a little Salt ; put thefe, with a moderate Quantity of Water, into a Kettle, and boil them for an Hour and an Half, and ftrain out the Liquor through a Sieve, and it will be a good Stock for Soops, either of Afparagus Buds, Lettuce, or any other kind fit for Lent or Faft-Days.

3 crusts of bread
Chervil, as needed
Beet, as needed
Swiss chard, as needed
Spinach, as needed
Celery, as needed
Leeks, as needed
Butter, as needed
Bunch of sweet herbs, as needed
Salt, to taste
Water, as needed

❖ *Using a large stock pot, combine chopped chervil, beets, Swiss chard, spinach, celery, leeks, a handful of herbs, salt, three slices of* **WHITE BREAD**, **BUTTER**, *and enough water to cover the vegetables. Bring to a boil. Reduce the temperature to medium-low and allow to simmer for 90 minutes. Strain through a fine wire sieve.*

➤ For vegetable stock: Using a large stock pot, combine four quarts of water, one-half cup of chopped onion, one-quarter cup each of chopped leeks, celery, carrots, and turnips, one garlic clove crushed, four each of parsley and thyme stems, one-quarter teaspoon of crushed black peppercorn, and one bay leaf. Bring to a boil. Reduce the temperature to medium-low and allow to simmer for 60 minutes. Strain through a fine wire sieve. Bottle and refrigerate.

The ingredients and quantities used for creating stocks varied by individual because the technique was done to the individual's preference or taste and not by availability of ingredients used.

Plants used in the recipes are winter hardy and would have been available year-round.

Herbs and spices are added to the water to provide flavor. A century later, these herbs are being held together using butchers' twine while the spices are contained in a cloth bag.

These two methods are referred to as:

- bouquet garni - herbs tied in a bundle containing parsley and thyme stems, leek, and celery leaf, and

- Sachet – spices contained in a cheesecloth bag containing black peppercorns, garlic clove, bay leaf, and cloves.

We also see the use of onions and celery in the stock; however, it would be a century later when this vegetable mixture would be called Mirepoix, a combination of diced onion, carrots, and celery.

Sauces

Chart of Modern Sauces

Béchamel

- Cream
- Mornay
- Soubise

Velouté

- Veal Velouté
- Chicken Velouté
- Fish Velouté
- Allemande or Mushroom
- Mushroom
- Anchovy

Espagnole

- Sauce Robert
- Mushroom
- Charcutière

Emusified

- Hollandaise

Brown Sauce.

Espagnole

Take a Lump of Butter, put it into the Saucepan, with a Pinch of Flour, and brown it; add fome Cives, Parfley, and Mufhrooms, all fhred very fmall, a few Capers, and an Anchovy, and feafon the Whole with Pepper and Salt, moiften it with a little Fifh-Broth, and thicken it with a Crawfifh, or other Cullis.

Mince fome Cives and Parfley ; fet a Sauce-pan over a Stove, with a Lump of frefh Butter, and melt it ; then put in a little Flour and brown it: when it is browned, put in the Cives and Parfley, together with Fifh-Broth, or Juice of Onions; feafon it with Salt and Pepper; let it fimmer awhile.

> Chives, as needed
> Parsley, as needed
> Butter, as needed
> Flour, as needed
> Fish Broth, as needed
> Salt, to taste
> Pepper, to taste

❖ *Mince chives and parsley and set aside. Melt a lump of* **BUTTER** *and stir in a little bread flour sautéing until well browned [stir the flour to keep it from burning while browning]. Stir in* **FISH STOCK**, *chives, and parsley seasoning with salt and ground black pepper.*

Here are two separate recipes for brown sauce using similar ingredients: butter, flour, chives, capers, salt, pepper, and fish broth. Alternate ingredients include onion and mushrooms.

The five common ingredients between a modern Espagnole [brown sauce] and recipes for brown sauce in the 18TH century include: flour, butter, broth, salt, and pepper. The basic process of making sauces has not changed in over 200 years.

A quick Espagnole can consist of one tablespoon each of melted **BUTTER** and flour. Stir the flour and butter together sautéing until well browned. Whisk in one cup of **BROWN STOCK** and bring to a boil. Add additional stock, or allow to simmer, so the sauce is the thickness of heavy cream. Season with salt and ground black pepper to taste.

Generally, brown sauce is made using brown stock; however, the writer of the recipe uses fish broth. Fish broth is also seen in a recipe for fish stock where the butter is browned for making brown stock suggesting the individual lived near water where fish was abundant.

The first recipe calls for the addition of mushrooms which would be equivalent to a modern-day mushroom sauce.

- For Espagnole: Melt three tablespoons of **BUTTER** in a sauté pan and stir in three tablespoons of bread flour sautéing until well browned [stir the flour to keep it from burning while browning]. Whisk two cups of **BROWN STOCK** and two tablespoons of tomato purée into the flour bringing to a boil. Add additional stock, or allow to simmer, so the sauce is the thickness of heavy cream. Season with salt and ground black pepper to taste.

Mufhroom Sauce.

Mushroom Sauce

CLEAN and wafh well a quart of frefh mufhrooms, cut them in two, and put them into a ftew pan, with a little falt, a blade of mace, and a little butter. Stew it gently for half an hour, and then add a pint of cream, and the yolks of two eggs beat very well. Keep ftirring it till it boil up, and then fqueeze in half a lemon. Put it over your fowls or turkies, or you may put it into bafons, or in a difh, with a piece of French bread firft buttered then toafted toafted brown, and juft dipped into boiling water. Put it in the difh, and mufhrooms over it. This is a very good fauce for white fowls of all forts.

> 1 quart mushrooms, cut in half
> Salt, to taste
> Mace, ground, to taste
> Butter, as needed
> 2 cups heavy cream

2 egg yolks, beaten
1/2 lemon, juiced
1 slice French bread, buttered and toasted
Water, as needed

❖ *Prepare the **18TH CENTURY BÉCHAMEL** omitting the nutmeg and pickled mushrooms. Sauté eight ounces of sliced mushrooms with one tablespoon of **BUTTER** until soft. Whisk in the 18TH century béchamel sauce and two egg yolks. Season with salt and ground mace to taste.*

In this recipe the writer toasts buttered bread until browned and dips it in boiling water. The bread will thicken the heavy cream in the sauce resembling a modern Béchamel which is added to sautéed mushrooms.

The recipe also incorporates egg yolks and lemon juice seen in modern Allemande sauce.

The modern equivalents for this 18TH century sauce are Allemande, Suprême, and Espagnole, each with sautéed mushrooms; however, none of these sauces appear for another century.

Allemande Sauce

➤ Prepare **VEAL VELOUTÉ** whisking in a scant one-quarter teaspoon of lemon juice, two tablespoons of heavy cream, and one egg yolk.

Mushroom Sauce I

➢ Prepare **ALLEMANDE** or **SUPRÊME** and set aside. Sauté four ounces of sliced mushrooms with one and one-half teaspoons of lemon juice and one tablespoon of **BUTTER** until soft. Combine the prepared sauce and mushrooms.

Mushroom Sauce II

➢ Prepare **ESPAGNOLE** and set aside. Sauté four ounces of sliced mushrooms with one tablespoon of shallots diced small and one tablespoon of **BUTTER** until the mushrooms are soft. Combine the Espagnole, onions, and mushrooms. Season with a few drops of lemon juice to taste.

Sauce Robert.

Sauce Robert

TAKE fome large onions, cut them into fquare pieces, and cut fome fat bacon in the fame manner. Put them together in a faucepan over the fire, and fhake them round to prevent their burning. When they be brown, put in fome good veal gravy, with a little pepper and falt, and let them ftew gently till the onions be tender. Then put in a little falt, fome muftard and vinegar, and ferve it hot.

Large onions, as needed
Bacon fat, as needed
Veal gravy, as needed

Salt, to taste
Pepper, to taste
Mustard powder, to taste
Vinegar, to taste

* *Sauté onions, diced large, with bacon fat, stirring occasionally, until browned. Add **VEAL STOCK** and allow to simmer until the onions are soft. Season with salt, mustard powder, and vinegar to taste.*

This recipe for sauce Robert is just a variant of an 18TH century onion sauce adding vinegar and mustard powder. This is really just sautéed onions rather than a sauce.

> For sauce Robert: Prepare **ESPAGNOLE** and set aside. Sauté one-quarter cup of onions, diced small, with one tablespoon of **BUTTER**, stirring occasionally, until the onions are opaque and not browned. Add one-half cup of **WHITE WINE** and allow to simmer until the wine has reduced two-thirds. Combine Espagnole and onion mixture whisking in one teaspoon of mustard powder, one-quarter teaspoon each of granulated sugar and lemon juice.

White Sauce.

Béchamel

TAKE the necks of fowls, a fcrag of veal, or any bits of mutton or veal you may have by you, and put them into a faucepan, with a blade or two of mace, a few black pepper-corns, an

anchovy, ahead of celery, a flice of the end of a lemon, and abunch of fweet herbs. Put to thefe a quart of water, cover it clofe, and let it boil till it be reduced to half a pint. Then ftrain it, and thicken it with a quarter of a pound of butter, mixed with flour, and boil it five or fix minutes. Then put in two fpoonfuls of pickled mufhrooms, and mix the yolks of two eggs with a tea-cupful of cream, and a little nutmeg grated. Put in your fauce, keep fhaking it over the fire, but take care that it does not boil. This is an excellent fauce for fowls.

Neck of fowl, as needed
Piece of veal, as needed
1/4 teaspoon mace, ground
Peppercorns, to taste
1 anchovy
1 head of celery
Lemon, 1 slice from end
4 cups water
4 ounces butter
Flour, as needed
2 tablespoons pickled mushrooms
2 egg yolks
4 ounces heavy cream
Nutmeg, ground, to taste

18TH Century Béchamel

❖ *Whisk together **BÉCHAMEL** and **VELOUTÉ** sauces, two egg yolks, and optional one-quarter cup of diced **PICKLED MUSHROOMS**. Some recipes did not mention pickled mushrooms.*

This white sauce recipe incorporates ingredients used in making three modern white sauces and one variation of a brown sauce that are not defined until the 19TH century:

- Stock from neck of veal-used for making Velouté,
- Dairy [cream]-used for making Béchamel and Suprême,
- Pickled mushrooms-used for making Charcutière where the mushrooms are replaced with sour pickles.

The main ingredient in the recipe that suggests it is Béchamel is the use of nutmeg.

Béchamel

➤ Melt three tablespoons of **BUTTER** and stir in three tablespoons of bread flour. Sauté until the flour starts to bubble and whisk in two cups of whole milk while bringing to a boil. Add additional milk, or allow to simmer, so the sauce is the thickness of heavy cream. Season with salt, ground white pepper, and ground nutmeg to taste.

Mornay

➤ Prepare **BÉCHAMEL** sauce whisking in two ounces of grated Gruyère cheese [substitute **CHEDDAR CHEESE**], four ounces of grated **PARMESAN CHEESE**, and two tablespoons of **BUTTER**. Continue to whisk until the butter and cheese are well combined. Whisk in enough milk thinning the sauce to the thickness of heavy cream.

Velouté

➢ Melt three tablespoons of **BUTTER** and stir in three tablespoons of bread flour. Sauté until the flour starts to bubble and whisk in two cups of **VEAL**, **CHICKEN**, or **FISH STOCK** while bringing to a boil. Add additional stock, or allow to simmer, so the sauce is the thickness of heavy cream. Season with salt and ground white pepper to taste.

Suprême

➢ Prepare **CHICKEN VELOUTÉ** whisking in one-half cup of heavy cream with two tablespoons of **BUTTER**. Season with salt, ground white pepper, and lemon juice to taste.

Charcutière

➢ For Charcutière: Prepare **SAUCE ROBERT** whisking in two tablespoons of minced **GERMAN PICKLES**.

Onion Sauce.

Soubise

THOUGH the directions given in the preceding article for making onion fauce may be fufficient, yet it may be expected that we fhould mention here the common method of making it. Boil eight or ten large onions, and change the water two or three times while they be boiling. When they be enough, chop them on a board, to prevent their growing of a bad colour, and put them into a faucepan with a quarter of a pound of butter, and two fpoonfuls of thick cream. Juft give them a boil up, and they will be done.

TAKE a Stew-pan, put into it fome Veal Gravy, with a Couple of Onions cut in Slices; feafon with Pepper and Salt, let it ftew foftly, then ftrain it off; put it in a Saucer, and ferve it up hot.

> Veal gravy, as needed
> 2 onions, sliced
> Pepper, to taste
> Salt, to taste

❖ *Place **VEAL STOCK** with two sliced onions in a sauce pot and season with salt and pepper to taste. Cook onions until soft. Drain and serve.*

> Prepare **BÉCHAMEL** and set aside. Sauté one large onion, diced small, with one tablespoon of **BUTTER**, stirring occasionally to prevent the onion from burning, until soft and not browned. Using a food processor, puree the onion with the Béchamel. Add additional milk as necessary, or allow the sauce to simmer, so the sauce is the thickness of heavy cream.

Anchovy Sauce.

Anchovy Sauce

PUT an anchovy into a pint of gravy, and a quarter of a pound of butter rolled in a little flour, and ftir all together till it boils. You may add, at your difcretion, a little juice of a lemon, catchup, red wine or walnut liquor. Plain butter melted thick, with a fpoonful of walnut pickle or catchup, is very good fauce ; but you may put as many things into fauces as you fancy.

1 anchovy
2 cups fish stock
4 ounces butter
Flour, as needed
Catchup, to taste

❖ *Melt eight tablespoons of* **BUTTER** *and stir in bread flour. Sauté until the flour starts to bubble. Whisk in two cups of* **FISH STOCK** *and the anchovy. If you desire, season the sauce with ketchup [***FISH***, **SOY** *or* **WORCESTERSHIRE SAUCE***], lemon juice, or* **RED WINE***.*

28

The catchup used in the recipe would have been what was readily available since the recipe doesn't specify which catchup to use to season the sauce.

- For Anchovy sauce: Prepare **FISH VELOUTÉ** whisking in one-half cup of **WORCESTERSHIRE SAUCE**. Allow the sauce to simmer over medium-low temperature until it has reduced one-third. Remove from the heat and whisk in one-half cup of heavy cream, two egg yolks, five tablespoons of **BUTTER**, and two ounces of anchovies. Whisk until the anchovies have dissolved or puree the sauce in a food processor.

To make Egg Sauce.
Hollandaise Sauce

BOIL two eggs hard, half chop the whites, then put in the yolks, chop them both together, but not very fine , put them into a quarter of a pound of good melted butter, and put it in a boat.

2 eggs, hard boiled
4 ounces butter, melted

- Coarsely chop two egg whites and add the yolks mincing the whites with the yolks. Melt eight tablespoons of **BUTTER** and whisk in the eggs.
    - To hard boil eggs: Place eggs into a sauce pot with enough water to cover them. Bring to a boil. Reduce the temperature to medium. Allow to

simmer for seven minutes. Drain the eggs using a colander. Place them in ice-water and allow to cool. When the eggs are cool to the touch, under cold running water, remove the shell from the eggs.

- For Hollandaise sauce: Melt five tablespoons of **BUTTER** and set aside. Using a double boiler: In the upper pot, whisk together four egg yolks with two tablespoons of water and one-half teaspoon of lemon juice. Fill the lower pot one-quarter full of water and bring to a boil. Place the upper pot onto the lower pot. Continually whisk the eggs until thickened. Remove the upper pot and slowly whisk in the melted butter. Whisk in enough boiling water to thin the Hollandaise to desired consistency, Season with salt to taste.

Cooking techniques and recipe ingredients varied greatly among individuals. Sauces were created by making a seasoned stock combined with flour for thickening all in one recipe. Today, stocks are prepared in advance for simple and quick production of sauces as needed.

In the 19TH century, Georges-Auguste Escoffier standardized the recipes for stocks and sauces; however, he is not the inventor. The five main standardized mother sauces are: Espagnole, Béchamel, Velouté, Tomato, and Hollandaise, with sub-variations of the sauces making it simple to learn and teach the cooking technique to aspiring chefs.

There is evidence that supports the beginning of these standard cooking techniques in the 17TH century that includes brown sauce [Espagnole], white sauce [Béchamel], and egg sauce [Hollandaise].

Velouté is a variation of Béchamel yet to be created. There were no tomato-based sauces during this period because tomatoes were considered poisonous.

Fruits and Salads

To Bake Apples Whole.
Baked Apples

PUT your Apples into an earthen Pan, with a few Cloves, and little Lemon-peel, fome coarfe Sugar, a Glafs of Red Wine; put them into a quick Oven, and they will take an Hour baking.

To Stew Pippins Whole.
Stewed Apples

TAKE twelve Golden Pippins, pare them, put the Parings into a Sauce-pan, with Water enough to cover them, a Blade of Mace, two or three Cloves, a Piece of Lemon-peal, let them fimmer till there is juft enough to ftew the Pippins in, then ftrain it, and put it into the Sauce-pan again, with Sugar enough to make it like a Syrup; then put them in a Preferving-pan, or clean Stew-pan, or large Sauce-pan, and pour the Syrup over them. Let there be enough to ftew them in; when they are enough, which you will know by the Pippins being foft, take them up, lay them in a little Difh with the Syrup; when cold, ferve them up; or hot, if you chufe it.

12 golden apples, pared
Water, as needed

Brown sugar, as needed
Pinch of ground mace
3 whole cloves
Lemon peel, grated

- ❖ *Peel 12 granny smith apples and set aside. Using a stock pot, combine the apple peels, three cloves, pinch of ground mace, and one tablespoon of grated lemon. Add one-half cup of water and bring to a boil. Reduce the temperature to medium and allow to simmer, while stirring, until the water has reduced by one-half. Strain through a fine sieve and return the water to the pot adding one-quarter cup of brown sugar. Bring to a hard boil. Add the apples and place a lid on the pot reducing the temperature to medium-low. Simmer the apples until they are al dente or fork tender turning the apples over during the cooking process allowing the apples to cook evenly. Allow to cool to room temperature. Plate pouring the sauce over the apples.*

- Apples appeared in Europe in the 12TH century.

- ➢ Alternate method: Use **RED WINE** instead of water and add two teaspoons of ground cinnamon.

- ➢ Alternate method: Serve the apples with a scoop of **VANILLA ICE-CREAM**.

Both recipes can be expanded into three additional modern recipes:

Fried Apples

➤ Peel and slice 12 Granny Smith apples into eight pieces, remove the core and seeds, and set aside. Using a stock pot, combine the apple peels, three cloves, pinch of ground mace, and one tablespoon of grated lemon. Add one-half cup of water and bring to a boil. Reduce the temperature to medium and allow to simmer, while stirring, until the water has reduced by one-half. Strain through a fine sieve and return the water to the pot adding one-half cup each of granulated sugar and water, one tablespoon each of cornstarch and melted **BUTTER**, one tablespoon of **ROSE WATER** or **FORTIFIED WINE**, two teaspoons of grated lemon peel, one-half teaspoon of ground cinnamon, and one-quarter teaspoon of ground mace. Bring to a hard boil. Reduce temperature to medium. Add the sliced apples and allow to simmer, while gently stirring, until they are al dente. Remove from heat and allow to cool, or

Applesauce

➤ Prepare **FRIED APPLES** and cover the pot. Continue to simmer, stirring occasionally, until the apples have broken down into a puree, or

Apple Butter

➤ Follow directions for **APPLESAUCE** removing the lid. Continue to simmer; stirring regularly to keep from burning the sauce, until sugar has caramelized and the color is deep dark brown.

To Stew Pears.

Poached Pears

PARE fix Pears, and either quarter them, or do them whole ; but makes a pretty Difh with one whole, and the other cut in quarter, and the Cores taken out, lay them in a deep earthen Pot, with a few Cloves, a Piece of Lemon-peel, a Gill of Red Wine, and a quarter of a Pound of fine Sugar: If the Pears are very large, they will take half a Pound of Sugar, and half a Pint of Red Wine. Cover them clofe with brown Paper, and bake them till they are enough. Serve them hot or cold, juft as you like them, and they will be very good with Water in the place of Wine.

> 6 pears, peeled
> Cloves, to taste
> Lemon peel, grated
> 5 ounces red wine
> 1/2 cup brown sugar

- Although pears date back to as early as 700 BC, cultivation of pears in Europe did not begin until the 17TH century.

- For poached pears: Peel six pears, cutting into quarters, and remove the core. Place the pears in an oven safe pot. Using a sauce pot, combine five ounces of **RED WINE**, one-half cup of brown sugar, eight whole cloves, and one tablespoon of grated lemon peel. Heat over medium temperature, stirring regularly, until the sugar has dissolved. Bring to a hard boil. Strain through a fine wire sieve. Pour the wine mixture over the pears and bake at 350°F until they are al dente or fork tender. Remove from oven and allow to cool to room temperature.

To Stew Pears in a Sauce-Pan.

Stewed Pears

PUT them into a Sauce-pan with the Ingredients as before. Cover them, and do them over a flow Fire; when they are enough take them off.

- ❖ *These are the same ingredients as the above* **POACHED PEARS**; *however, the pears are cooked in a sauté pan until done to taste.*

- ➢ For stewed pears: Peel and slice each pear into eight pieces removing the core and set aside. Using a sauce pot, combine one-half cup each of **RED WINE** and brown sugar, eight whole cloves, and one tablespoon of grated lemon peel. Heat over medium temperature, stirring regularly, until the sugar has dissolved. Bring to a hard boil. Strain through a fine wire sieve. Return the wine to the pot adding the pears. Simmer the pears over medium heat, stirring occasionally, until they al dente or fork tender. Remove from heat and allow to cool to room temperature.

Other Grand Sallets.

Basic Salad

Take green purslain and pick it leaf by leaf, wash it and swing it in a napkin, then being disht in a fair clean dish, and finely piled up in a heap in the midst of it lay round about the centre of the sallet pickled capers, currans, and raisins of the sun, washed, pickled, mingled, and laid round it: about them some carved cucumbers in slices or halves , and laid round also. Then garnish the dish brims with borage, or clove jelly-flowers. Or otherways with jagged cucumber-peels, olives, capers, and raisins of the sun, then the best sallet-oyl and wine-vinegar.

>   Purslane [substitute spinach], as needed
>   Capers, as needed
>   Currants [substitute raisins], as needed
>   Raisins, as needed
>   Cucumber, sliced
>   Borage [substitute mint], as needed

- Salads date back to the Roman Empire consisting of raw vegetables with a salt and oil dressing.

Basic Salad Oil

> ➢ Basic salad oil and vinegar dressing is one-part **VINEGAR** to three parts oil. Pour the vinegar and oil into a blender and blend until the oil starts to turn white or cloudy. Season with salt

and ground black pepper to taste.

➢ For basic salad: In a bowl, toss together two ounces of spinach and one-half ounce of mint leaves. Drizzle with two tablespoons of **BASIC SALAD OIL** and toss evenly coating the leaves. Garnish with two tablespoons of capers, six olives, 12 raisins, and six cucumber slices one-quarter inch thick.

Other Grand Sallets.

Other Basic Salad

All sorts of good herbs, the little leaves of red sage, the smallest leaves of sorrel, and the leaves of parsley pickt very small, the youngest and smallest leaves of spinage, some leaves of burnet, the smallest leaves of lettice, white endive and charvel all finely pick't and washed, and swung in a strainer or clean napkin, and well drained from the water; then dish it in a clean scowred dish, and about the centre capers, currans, olives, lemons carved and slic't, boil'd beet-roots carved and slic't, and dished round also with good oyl and vinegar.

Red sage leaves [substitute common sage], as needed
Sorrel [substitute arugula], as needed
Parsley, as needed
Spinach, as needed
Burnet [substitute mint], as needed
Romaine lettuce, as needed

White endive, as needed
Chervil [substitute parsley], as needed
Capers, as needed
Currants [substitute raisins], as needed
Olives, as needed
Lemons, sliced, as needed
Beet root, cooked, as needed

> For other basic salad: In a bowl, toss together one ounce each of chopped romaine lettuce, endive, arugula, and spinach, one tablespoon each of minced parsley, sage, and minced mint leaves. Dress the salad with two tablespoons of **BASIC SALAD OIL** and toss evenly coating the ingredients. Divide the salad into two individual bowls. Garnish each salad with two tablespoon of capers, six olives, 12 raisins, six slices of cooked beet one-quarter inch thick and garnished with one lemon wedge on the side.

Soups and Broth

Beef broth.

Beef Soup

PUT a leg of beef into a pot with a gallon of water, having firſt waſh'ed the beef clean, and cracked the one in two or three parts. Skim it well, and put in two or three blades of mace, a little bundle of parſley, and a large cruſt of bread. Let it boil till the beef and the finews be quite tender cut fome toaſted bread into dice, and put it into your tureen. Then lay in the meat, and pour in the foup.

1 gallon water
1 leg of beef, broken into three parts
Three blades ground mace
Handful of fresh parsley
Bread, crust
Bread, diced and toasted

It was common in the 18TH century to write one recipe having multiple procedures as seen in this recipe.

    I.   The first procedure is to create a broth, while

    II. the second procedure is to assemble the soup.

The writer is calling the recipe a broth; however, at the end of the recipe, a soup has been prepared. It wasn't until a century later that the one procedure would be separated into two recipes.

- Soups date back to Ancient Greece consisting of pork, pork blood, and vinegar.

- For beef soup: Purchase beef shanks or oxtail. Using a stock pot, combine the beef with 12 ounces of **BROWN STOCK** for each shank or oxtail purchased. Simmer over medium temperature until the beef is tender and easily pulls away from the bone and the stock has reduced one-third. Season with salt, ground black pepper, and ground mace to taste. Pull the meat off each bone serving in a bowl with eight ounces of stock drawn from the bottom of the pot. Garnish with fresh chopped parsley.

White foup.

Bisque

PUT a knuckle of veal into fix quarts of water, with a large fowl, and a pound of lean bacon ; half a pound of rice, two anchovies, a few pepper-corns, a bundle of fweet herbs, two or three onions, and three or four heads of celery cut in flices. Stew them all together, till the foup be as ftrong as you would have it, and then ftrain it through a hair fieve into a clean earthen pot. Having let it ftand all night, the next day take off the fcum, and pour it clear off into a toffing-pan. Put in half a pound of

Jordan almonds beat fine, boil it a little, and run it through a lawn fieve. Then put in a pint of cream, and the yolk of an egg, and fend it up hot.

> 1 knuckle of veal
> 1 chicken, parted
> 6 quarts water
> 1 pound bacon
> 1 cup Arborio rice
> 2 anchovies
> Peppercorns, as needed
> Bundle of sweet herbs
> 2 onions
> 3 celery heads, sliced
> 1/2-pound almonds, ground
> 2 cups heavy cream
> 1 egg yolk

The term white soup tends to be very broad. You can have white bean soup, white chicken soup, or even white fish soup. The possibilities are almost endless.

In this recipe, the starch from the rice along with the egg yolk will thicken the bisque; whereas, a sauce is used in a modern bisque.

This recipe incorporates ingredients used in making two modern soups and a bisque that are not defined until the 19TH century: Clear soup, cream soup, and bisque.

Clear Soup

> Prepare **VEAL, CHICKEN,** or **VEGETABLE STOCK.**

Cream Soup

> Prepare either **VEAL** or **CHICKEN VELOUTÉ** or **BÉCHAMEL.** Melt one tablespoon of **BUTTER** and whisk with one cup of milk into the desired prepared sauce.

Bisque

> Prepare **FISH STOCK** and **FISH VELOUTÉ.** Whisk together two cups of Velouté, one cup of fish stock, and one-half cup of heavy cream.

Adding in other ingredients

White Bean Soup

> Prepare **CLEAR SOUP** adding four ounces of diced ham, one head of crushed garlic, and eight ounces of canned navy beans. Season with salt and ground black pepper to taste.

White Chicken Soup

> Prepare **CREAM SOUP** adding four ounces of chicken medium diced, one clove of crushed garlic, and one-half teaspoon each of cumin and coriander. Allow to simmer until chicken is

cooked through. Remove from heat and whisk in two tablespoons of **CRÈME FRAÎCHE**. Season with salt and ground white pepper to taste.

Mushroom Soup

➤ Alternate method: Use sliced mushrooms in place of chicken.

Shrimp Bisque

➤ Prepare **BISQUE** adding a pinch of dried thyme, one-quarter teaspoon dried parsley, one and one-half teaspoons of tomato paste, three ounces of **WHITE WINE**, six ounces of fresh whole shrimp, one tablespoon each of onion and carrot, diced small. Cook the bisque over medium temperature until the shrimp has turned red. Strain the bisque through a colander, saving the shrimp and reserving the liquid. Peel, devein, and medium dice the shrimp. Combine the liquid and shrimp, season with salt and white pepper to taste.

Common peas foup.

Pea Soup

PUT four quarts of foft water to one quart of fplit peas, with a little lean bacon, or roaft-beef bones; wafh a head of celery, cut it, and put it in, with a turnip. Boil it till it be reduced to two quarts, and then work it through a cullender with a wooden fpoon. Mix a little flour and water, and boil it well in the foup. Slice in another head of celery, and feafon it to your tafle with falt and chyan pepper. Cut a dice of bread into fmall dice, and fry them of a light brown. Put them into your difh, and pour your foup over them.

4 quarts water
1 quart split peas
Bacon, as needed
2 heads of celery, chopped
Turnip, chopped
Flour, as needed
Salt, to taste
Cayenne pepper, to taste
Bread, sliced and toasted

> For pea soup: Using a stock pot, combine two quarts of **VEAL STOCK** with one ham hock. Heat over medium temperature until the stock has reduced one-half. Add one-half head of chopped celery. Reduce the temperature to medium-low and allow to simmer until the celery is al dente. Add two cups of fresh peas [substitute frozen peas] and continue to simmer until the peas start to shrivel. Remove the ham hock and puree the peas, celery, and stock in a blender. For a smooth sauce, pass the puree through a fine wire sieve. Return the puree to the pot. Season with salt and cayenne pepper to taste.

White onion foup.

Cream of Onion Soup

BOIL thirty large onions in five quarts of water, with a knuckle of veal, a little whole pepper, and a blade or two of mace. Take your onions up as foon as they be quite foft, rub them through a hair fieve, and work into them half a pound of butter, with fome flour. When the meat be boiled off the bones, ftrain the liquor to the onions, and boil it gently for half an hour, and then ferve it up, with a large cupful of cream, and a little falt. Be careful not to fuffer it to burn when you put in the flour and butter, which may be prevented by ftirring it well.

30 onions
5 quarts of water
1 knuckle of veal
Peppercorn, as needed
2 blades ground mace
8 ounces butter, room temperature
Flour, as needed
1 cup cream
Salt, to taste

❖ *Using a stock pot, combine 30 onions, five quarts of water, a knuckle of veal, pepper, and one-quarter teaspoon of ground mace. Bring to a boil. Reduce the temperature to medium-low and allow to simmer until the onions are soft. Using a food processor, puree the onions. Return the onions to the pot. Add eight ounces of* **BUTTER** *and some bread flour. Strain the* *water into the onions and boil for 30 minutes. Serve with a cup of heavy cream and salt.*

> For onion soup: Using a sauce pot, combine one pound of onions cut into thin pieces with two tablespoons of **BUTTER**. Sauté the onions, stirring occasionally to keep from burning, until they are opaque. Stir in two tablespoons of bread flour. Whisk in four cups of **VEAL** or **CHICKEN STOCK**. Bring to a boil. Using a blender, puree the soup. For a smooth soup, pass the puree through a fine wire sieve. Return the soup to the pot and whisk in one-quarter cup of heavy cream. Season with salt, ground mace, and ground black pepper to taste.

> Alternate method: Using a sauce pot, combine one pound of onions cut into thin pieces with two tablespoons of **BUTTER**. Sauté the onions, stirring occasionally to keep from burning, until they have browned. Add two cups of **BROWN STOCK**. Bring to a boil. Remove from heat and season with salt and ground black pepper to taste. Optional: Divide the soup equally into bowls. Slice and toast a baguette. Top the soup with two slices of toasted baguette and grated gruyere cheese placing under a broiler until the cheese has melted.

Egg foup.
Egg Soup

HAVING beaten the yolks of two eggs in a difh, with a piece of butter as big as a hen's egg, take

a tea-kettle of boiling-water in one hand, and a fpoon in the other. Pour in about a quart by degrees, then keep ftirring it all the time well till the eggs are well mixed, and the butter melted. Then pour it into a fauce-pan, and keep ftirring it all the time till it begin to fimmer. take it off the fire, and pour it between two veffels, out of one into another, till it be quite fmooth, and has a great froth. Set it on the fire again, keep ftirring it till it be quite hot, then pour it into, your foup-difh, and fend it hot to table.

2 eggs, separated
4 ounces butter, room temperature
6 cups boiling water

- ❖ Place four cups of **VEGETABLE STOCK** into a sauce pot. Whisk together four egg yolks and eight tablespoons of soft **BUTTER**, setting aside. Bring the stock to a boil. While briskly whisking the egg yolk, temper it by slowly adding the hot stock. Return the stock to the pot. Using medium-high heat, whisk until the soup begins to boil and remove from heat. Season with salt to taste.
- ➢ For egg soup, prepare **HOLLANDAISE** and whisk in four cups of boiling **VEGETABLE STOCK**.

This is not an Asian egg-drop soup. In this recipe the egg is tempered with boiling water; where, with Asian egg drop soup, the egg is whisk into hot stock.

Beef

Beef efcarlot. Another Way.
Corned Beef

TAKE a Brifcuit of Beef, half a Pound of coarfe Sugar, two Ounces of Bay Salt, a Pound of common Salt, mix all together, and rub the Beef, lay it in an Earthen Pan, and turn it every Day. It may lie a Fortnight in the Pickle, then boil it, and ferve it up either with Savoys, or a Peas-pudding.

>1 whole brisket
>1 pound salt
>1 cup brown sugar
>2 ounces bay salt

- ❖ *For a curing rub, combine two cups of canning and pickling salt, one cup of brown sugar, and one-quarter cup of sea salt. Evenly coat the brisket with curing rub. Place the brisket onto a baker's sheet pan and refrigerate. Turn the brisket over once per day for 14 days. Place the brisket in a large stock pot with enough water to cover. Bring to a boil. Reduce the temperature to medium and allow to simmer until the internal temperature of the brisket reaches 155°F.*

- ➢ For corned beef: Dissolve one-quarter cup of Morton® Tender Quick® with two cups of canning and pickling salt into one gallon of hot water. Allow to cool to room temperature. Place the brine and brisket in a large container. Weight the brisket to keep it below the water line adding additional brine as necessary. Refrigerate the brisket for 14 days turning once per day. After 14 days, rinse the brisket with warm water to remove any excess salt. Preheat oven to 260°F and bake until the internal temperature of the brisket reaches 155°F.

- ➢ Alternate method: Follow the directions on your smoker and smoke the brisket until internal temperature reaches 155°F.

- • Pastrami originated from the town of Pastirma, Turkey during the 13th century.

Pastrami

- ➢ Combine one-quarter cup of ground black pepper, two tablespoons of ground coriander seed, one tablespoon each of brown sugar, paprika, garlic powder, and onion powder, and one and one-half teaspoons of mustard powder. Evenly coat the brisket with the spice mixture. Follow the directions on your smoker and smoke the brisket until internal temperature reaches 155°F.

Veal Cutlets.
Country Fried Steak

CUT your veal into pieces about the thicknefs

of half a crown, and as long as you pleafe. Dip them in the yolk of an egg, and ftrew over them crumbs of bread, a few fweet herbs, fome lemon-peel, and a little grated nutmeg, and fry them in frefh butter. While they are frying, make a little gravy, and when the meat be done, take it out, and-lay it in a difh before the fire; then fhake a little flour into the pan, and ftir it round. Put in a little gravy, fqueeze in a little lemon, and pour it over the veal. Make ufe of lemon for your garnifh.

Veal cutlet, 1/2 inch thick
Egg yolk, beaten
Lemon, cut in slices
Gravy, as needed
Butter, as needed
Flour, as needed
Bread crumbs, as needed
Herbs, minced as needed
Lemon peel, grated as needed
Nutmeg, as needed

- A British Crown [coin] measured about one-inch in diameter.

When recipes call for the thickness of half a crown, the thickness would be about one-half inch.

Most countries have their own variation of this recipe:

  - France - Veal Francaise,
  - Germany - Jägerschnitzel,

- Italy - Scaloppine di vitello al Marsala.

➤ For country fried steak: In a stock pot, place fry oil to a one-inch depth and heat to 350°F.

Create a breading station using three bowls:

- In bowl one, combine one cup of unseasoned breadcrumbs, one tablespoon each of salt and grated lemon peel, one teaspoon each of dried parsley, marjoram, basil, oregano, and rubbed sage, one-half teaspoon of ground nutmeg, and one-quarter teaspoon of ground thyme.

- In bowl two, whisk together one-half cup of milk with one egg or use heavy whipping cream.

- In bowl three, place one-half cup of bread flour replacing as needed.

For the veal to fry evenly and remain tender, instead of one-half inch thick cut as directed in the recipe, pound the cutlet into one-quarter inch thick pieces. Coat the cutlet with flour shaking off excess. Dip the cutlet in milk and egg mixture, or heavy cream, and evenly coat with the seasoned breadcrumbs. Fry the cutlet in oil until golden brown on both sides and the internal temperature reaches 155°F. Plate the cutlet over **VELOUTÉ** and garnish with fresh minced parsley.

➤ Alternate method: Replace Velouté with **BÉCHAMEL** omitting the nutmeg and replacing it with ground black pepper to taste.

Veal Francaise

> Add one-quarter cup of **WHITE WINE** to the **VELOUTÉ** for French Veal Francaise, or

German Jägerschnitzel

> Replace the Velouté with **MUSHROOM SAUCE II** seasoning with two tablespoons of balsamic vinegar, or to taste, for German Jägerschnitzel, or

Scaloppinedi Vitello al Marsala

> Replace the balsamic vinegar in German Jägerschnitzel with two tablespoons of Marsala wine, or to taste, for Italian scaloppine di vitello al Marsala.

To Roast Beef.

Roast Beef

The general rules are, to have a brisk hot fire, to hang down rather than to spit, to baste with salt and water, and one quarter of an hour to every pound of beef, tho' tender beef will require less, while old tough beef will require more roasting; pricking with a fork will determine you whether done or not; rare done is the healthiest and the taste of this age.

Beef bottom round, netted for hanging
Water, as needed
Salt, as needed

This recipe would work best in a fireplace setting instead of an open fire. Using an open fire can be useful when cooking well to rare meat. The meat closest to the heat source will cook well where the meat farthest from the source, or in the center of the cut, will be rare. Using a fireplace setting, the radiant heat will cook the meat evenly similar to a convection oven.

- For roast beef: Create a brine by dissolving one-half cup of non-iodized salt in eight cups of hot water. Allow to cool to room temperature. Place the bottom round and brine into a ziplock bag. Allow to rest for two hours. Remove the round and rinse with water to remove any excess salt. Preheat an oven to 225°F and allow the round to bake until internal temperature reaches 130°F. Wrap the beef in aluminum foil and allow to rest for 15 minutes before slicing. Slice and serve over **ESPAGNOLE**.

- Alternate method: Instead of baking the round in an oven, follow the directions on your smoker and smoke the round until internal temperature reaches 130°F.

Beef Steaks.

Grilled Steak

THE beft beef fteaks are thofe cut off a rump, and fhould not be more than half an inch in thicknefs. Rub the gridiron with beef fuet, and let the fire be clear. When the gridiron be hot, lay your fteaks on it, and let them broil till they begin to look brown. Then turn them, and when the other fide be brown, lay them on a hot difh, with a flice of butter between each fteak, and fprinkle a little pepper and falt over them. Let them ftand two or three minutes, and in the mean time flice a fhalot, as thin as poffible, into a fpoonful of water. Lay your fteaks again on the gridiron, and keep them turning, till they be enough. Put them on your difh, pour the water and fhalot among them, and ferve them up.

Steak, 1 inch thick
Salt, as needed
Pepper, as needed
Butter, as needed
1 clove shallot, thin sliced
1 tablespoon water

This is a simple grilling recipe that we use today in the restaurant industry. Steaks are par-grilled [or marked] and topped with butter to be finished in a broiler when ordered by the guest.

- For grilled steak: Start by preheating a grill. While the grill is heating, season the steak with salt and ground black pepper allowing the steak to come to room temperature before grilling. Sauté one shallot sliced into thin pieces with one tablespoon of **BUTTER** until soft and set aside. When the grill is hot and the steak is at room temperature, grill turning one time [approximately seven minutes per side], or until done to taste. Top with butter and shallot, wrap in foil, and allow to rest for 15 minutes. This allows the moisture in the steak to distribute evenly.

Chicken

Chickens.

Chicken in Mushroom Sauce

HAVING flitted your chickens down the back, feafon them with pepper and falt, and lay them on the gridiron, over a clear fire, and at a great diftance. Let the infide continue next the fire till it be nearly half done. Then turn them, taking care that the flefhy fides do not burn, and let them broil till they are of a fine brown. Have good gravy fauce, with fome mufhrooms, and garnifh them with lemon and the liver broiled, and the gizzards cut, flafhed, and broiled, with pepper and falt; or you may ufe any other fauce you fancy.

> Chicken, cleaned and halved
> Salt, to taste
> Pepper, to taste
> Gravy, as needed
> Mushrooms, sliced
> Lemon, as needed

> For chicken in mushroom sauce: Prepare **MUSHROOM SAUCE I** or **MUSHROOM SAUCE II** and allow to simmer while the chicken is grilling. While preheating a grill, clean the chicken and separate by cutting it down the middle. Brush the chicken with vegetable oil and season with salt and ground black pepper. Place the chicken

on the grill bone side up. When the chicken is one-half done, turn it over and cook until the internal temperature reaches 165°F. Serve the chicken bone side down topped with mushroom sauce.

A MARINADE of Chickens.
Fried Chicken

Cut the chickens into quarters, and marinade them in the juice of lemons and verjuice, or with vinegar, falt, clove, pepper, chibols : or a bay leaf or two : Let them lie in this marinade for the fpace of three hours, then having made a fort of clear pafte or batter with flour, white wine and the yolks of three eggs, drop the chickens into it, then fry them in lard, and ferve them up in the form of a pyramid, with fry'd parfley and flices of lemon.

Whole chicken, cleaned and quartered
Parsley, as needed
Lemon, sliced, as needed

Marinade:
Verjuice or vinegar, as needed
Lemon juice, to taste
Salt, to taste
Clove, to taste
Pepper, to taste
Chibols or bay leaf, as needed

Paste:
Flour, as needed
White wine, as needed
3 eggs, yolks and whites separated
Lard for frying

- ❖ *For the marinade, whisk together two cups of **VINEGAR**, one tablespoon each of lemon juice, salt, ground black pepper, and one teaspoon of ground clove. Place the chicken pieces and marinade in a zip-lock bag refrigerating for one hour. After one hour: in a stock pot, add fry oil to one inch in depth and heat to 350°F. While the oil is heating, make a batter by whisking together one cup of bread flour, one and one-quarter cups of **white wine**, and three egg yolks. Remove the chicken from the marinade and pat dry. Dredge each piece of chicken in plain flour shaking off excess. Evenly coat each piece of chicken in the batter and fry until the chicken is golden brown on both sides and the internal temperature of the chicken reaches 165°F.*

For a crispy chicken, fry the battered chicken in oil until light brown. Remove and allow to cool, about 5 minutes. Refry in oil until medium brown and crispy and internal temperature reaches 165°F.

- ➢ Alternate method: Add one tablespoon each of salt and ground black pepper, one and one-half teaspoons each of garlic powder, onion powder, and paprika, and three-quarters teaspoon of cayenne pepper to the batter.

59

Depending on the cut of a chicken, each piece will cook longer than others. To keep from overcooking, clean and portion the chicken into eight pieces [two each: breast, thigh, drum, and leg].

> For fried chicken: Create a breading station using two bowls:

- In bowl one, combine one cup of bread flour, one tablespoon each of salt and ground black pepper, one and one-half teaspoons each of garlic powder, onion powder, and paprika, and three-quarters teaspoon of cayenne pepper.

- In bowl two, whisk together one cup of milk with two eggs or use heavy cream.

Dredge the chicken in the flour mixture shaking off excess. Coat the chicken in the milk mixture and again, dredge in the flour mixture. Deep fry until golden brown and the internal temperature reaches 165°F.

> Alternate method: Steam the chicken for 15 minutes seasoning with salt and ground black pepper prior to breading and frying.

Pulled Chicken.

Chicken in White Wine & Cream

BOIL fix chickens till they be nearly enough; then flea them, and pull the white flefh all off from the bones. Put it in a ftew-pan, with half a pint of cream made fcalding hot, the gravy

that ran from the chickens, and a few fpoonfuls of the liquor they were boiled in. To this add fome raw parfley fhred fine, and give the whole a tofs or two over the fire duft a little flour over a piece of butter, and fhake them up. Chickens done this way muft be killed the night before, and a little more than half boiled, and pulled in pieces as broad as your finger, and half as long. You may add a fpoonful of white wine to the above ingredients.

> Chicken, cooked and pulled
> Flour, as needed
> 8 ounces heavy cream
> Fresh parsley, minced as needed
> Butter, as needed
> 1 Tablespoon white wine
> Water, as needed

- ❖ *Using a stock pot, combine the chicken with enough water to cover. Bring to a boil. Allow to boil until the internal temperature of the chicken reaches 165°F. Drain the chicken using a colander and shred into pieces. Using a sauce pot, combine the chicken with one cup of cream, minced parsley, and one tablespoon of* **BUTTER** *coated with bread flour. Bring to a boil while whisking the butter and bread flour into the cream.*

- ➢ For chicken in white wine and cream: Preheat a grill. Clean a whole chicken and separate it by cutting it down the middle. While the grill is heating, prepare **SUPRÊME** whisking in one-quarter cup of **WHITE WINE**. Allow to simmer while the chicken is grilling. Brush the chicken with vegetable oil and season with salt and ground black pepper. When the grill is hot, place chicken on the grill bone side up. When one-half cooked, turn it over and cook until the internal temperature reaches 165°F. Serve the chicken over the sauce garnishing with minced parsley.

- Scottish and German settlers brought traditions with them to the new world. These are two earliest known sauces introduced in the middle of the 18TH century:

  - vinegar sauce brought by Scottish settlers,
  - mustard sauce brought by German settlers.

Barbecue Chicken

> Grill the chicken and shred into pieces. Using a sauce pot, whisk together one-half cup of brown sugar or one-quarter cup of molasses, one cup of **VINEGAR**, one teaspoon of cayenne pepper, and two teaspoons each of salt and ground black pepper. Allow to simmer until the brown sugar has dissolved. Remove from heat and allow to cool. For the mustard sauce, whisk in one-quarter cup of prepared mustard. Toss shredded chicken or pulled pork into one of the two sauces.

Chickens.

Chicken Fricassee

HAVING fkinned your chickens, and cut them into fmall pieces, wafh them in warm water, and dry them very clean with a cloth. Seafon them with falt and pepper, and put them into a ftew-pan with a little water, a large piece of butter, a bunch of thyme, and fweet marjoram, an onion ftuck with cloves, half a lemon, or a little lemon-pickle, a glafs of wine, an anchovy, and a little mace and nutmeg. Let them ftew till the chickens be tender, and then lay them on your difh. Having thickened your gravy with butter and flour, drain it, and then beat up the yolks of three eggs, and mix them with a gill of rich cream. Put this into your gravy, and fhake it over the fire, without fuffering it to boil. Pour this over your chickens, and ferve them up.

Chicken, skinned, bones removed, diced small
Salt, as needed
Pepper, as needed
Butter, as needed
Thyme, small handful
Marjoram, small handful
1 onion, peeled
Cloves, as needed
Lemon, cut in half
8 ounces white wine
1 anchovy
Mace, to taste
Nutmeg, to taste

Flour, as needed
3 eggs, separated
5 ounces heavy cream

- ❖ *Start by cleaning and separating a whole chicken into eight pieces [two each: breast, thigh, wing, drum], removing the bones, and medium dicing the chicken parts. Season the chicken with salt and pepper placing in a sauce pot with enough water to cover. Add **BUTTER**, thyme, sweet marjoram, an onion stuck with cloves, half of lemon, eight ounces of **WHITE WINE**, one anchovy, mace, and nutmeg. Simmer until the internal temperature of the chicken reaches 165°F. Remove the chicken and thicken the water with **BUTTER** and bread flour. Strain the sauce through a fine sieve. Whisk in three eggs and five ounces of heavy cream. Serve the chicken with the sauce spooned over it.*

- ➤ For chicken fricassee: Separate a whole chicken into eight pieces [2 wings, 2 thighs, 2 breasts, 2 drums]. Prepare **ALLEMANDE** and allow to simmer. Melt two tablespoons of **BUTTER** in a sauté pan and add the chicken parts searing on both sides but not browning. When the chicken is seared, add the Allemande and cover the pot. Reduce the temperature to medium-low and allow to simmer until the internal temperature of the chicken reaches 165°F. Remove the chicken and plate spooning the sauce over the chicken.

Pork

Pork Chops.

Pork Chops Robert

THE fame rules we have laid down for broiling mutton, will hold good with refpect to pork chops, with this difference only, that pork requires more broiling than mutton. As foon as they be enough, put a little good gravy to them, and drew a little fage, rubbed fine over them, which will give them an agreeable flavour.

Pork chops
Whole leaf sage, as needed
Sauce Robert, as needed

- *Start by preheating a grill. Place the pork on the grill turning once during the cooking time. While the pork is cooking, prepare gravy and allow to simmer until the pork is cooked to an internal temperature of 145°F. Remove the pork and rub fresh sage leaves across the top discarding the leaves when finished rubbing. Serve pork over gravy.*

> For pork chops Robert: Start by preheating a grill. Prepare **SAUCE ROBERT** and allow to simmer while pork is cooking. Brush the pork with oil and season with salt and ground black pepper. When the grill is hot, place the pork on the grill turning once [about seven minutes per side], until the pork has reached an internal temperature of 140°F. Remove the pork from

the grill and rub fresh sage leaves across the top by placing the sage leaves on the pork and using the palm of your hand rubbing back and forth. Discard the leaves when finished. Serve pork over sauce Robert.

To make Saufages, from Lady M.
Cumberland Sausage

TAKE the Flefh of a Leg of Pork, and mince it fmall, and to every Pound of the Flefh minced, mince about a quarter of a Pound of the hard Fat of the Hog then beat fome Jamaica pepper very fine, and mix with it fome Pepper and Salt, with a little Sweet Marjoram powder'd, and fome Leaves of red Sage minced very fmall; mix all thefe very well, and if you fill them into Guts, either of Hogs or Sheep, beat two or three Yolks of Eggs and mix with them, taking care not to fill the Guts too full, left they burft when you broil or fry them : but if you defign them to be eaten without putting them in Guts, then put no Eggs to them, but beat the Flefh and the Fat in a Stone Mortar, and work the Spice and Herbs well into it with your hands, fo that it be well mix'd, and keep it in a Mafs to ufe at your pleafure, breaking off Pieces, and rolling them in your hands, and then flowering them well before you fry them. If you ufe them in Guts, take fpecial care that the Guts are well clean'd, and lie fome time in a little warm White-wine and Spice before you ufe them ; if any Herb happens to be difagreeable in this Mixture, it may be left out, or others added at pleafure.

1 pound pork, chicken, or beef
Pepper, as needed
Salt, as needed
Marjoram, as needed
Sage, as needed
Intestines, as needed
2-3 egg yolks

➢ For Cumberland sausage: Start with two pounds of ground pork leg and thoroughly mix in two teaspoons of dried sage, three teaspoons of non-iodized salt, two teaspoons of ground black pepper, one teaspoon each of marjoram, ground thyme, and ground allspice [Jamaica pepper]. Stuff a hog's casing [intestine] with the ground pork and tie [twist] off every six inches.

➢ Alternate method: Hand pat sausage into three-inch round patties.

Options for cooking include pan frying, grilling, or smoking.

To do a Leg of Pork Ham Fafhion.
Cured Ham

TAKE a Leg of Pork, and let it be cut like a Ham; then take a Quart of ordinary Salt, and a Quart of Bay-falt, and heat it very hot, then mix it with a Pound of coarfe Sugar, and an Ounce of Salt-petre beaten fine, and rub the Ham well with it, and cover it all over with what is left, for it muft all go on, fo let it lie three Days; then turn it every Day for a Fortnight; then take it out, and fmoak it as you do Bacon or Tongues : The Salt muft be put on as hot as you can.

> 1 leg of pork
> 2 cups salt
> 2 cups bay-salt
> 1 pound sugar
> 1 ounce salt petre

> For cured ham: Prepare a basic dry cure by combining two cups of canning and pickling salt, two cups of granulated sugar, and two tablespoons of Morton® Tender Quick®. Weigh a pork leg and measure two tablespoons of cure for every pound. Evenly coat the leg with the cure. Put a cooling rack on top of a sheet pan and place the leg onto the cooling rack. Refrigerate and allow to rest for seven days. After seven days, remove the salt from the leg and evenly coat a second time with the dry cure. Return the leg to the refrigerator and allow to rest for 14 days. Place the leg in a stock pot with enough water to cover. Bring to a boil. Reduce the temperature to medium and continue to boil the leg until internal temperature reaches 145°F. Remove the leg and pat dry. Return the leg to the refrigerator for seven days.

I. If dry aging, tightly wrap the leg in fine woven cheese cloth and hang the ham in a well-ventilated room with low humidity at 70°F for 90 days.

II. If smoking, cold smoke the ham at 90°F for eight hours and hang the ham in a well-ventilated room with low humidity at 70°F for 90 days.

Fish

To marinate Salmon to be eaten either hot or cold.

Salmon

TAKE a Salmon, cut it into Joles and Rands, and fry them in Sallad Oil, or clarified Butter, then fet them by, then put into a Pipkin as much Claret and Wine Vinegar as will be fufficient to cover them ; put in a Faggot of fweet Herbs, as Rofemary, Thyme, Sweet Marjoram, Winter-Savoury, Parfley, Sage, Sorrel and Bay Leaves, Salt, grofs Pepper, Nutmeg, and Ginger fliced, large Mace and Cloves, bail all thefe well together; lay your Salmon into a Pan, and all being cold, pour this Liquor over it, lay on fliced Lemons and Lemon-peel, and cover it up clofe ; and you may either ferve it hot or cold, with the fame Liquor it was foufed in, with Spices, Herbs, and Lemons on it.

Salmon filet
Salad oil, as needed
Apples, as needed
Butter, as needed
Red wine, as needed
Wine vinegar, as needed
Handful of herbs: rosemary, thyme, marjoram, savory, parsley, sage, sorrel, bay leaves
Salt, to taste
Pepper, to taste
Mace, sliced

Cloves, to taste
Lemon, sliced
Grated lemon peel

Here we see the use of both the bouquet garni and sachet that are not defined until a century later.

- ❖ For salmon: Clean and filet a whole salmon cutting into four-ounce pieces. Prepare **BASIC SALAD OIL** for marinade. Place the salmon and marinade in a zip-lock bag and allow to marinate for one hour. Peel and core one GrannySmith apple and slice into eight pieces. Using a sauce pot, combine one cup of **RED WINE** with three sprigs each of thyme, parsley, and marjoram, one sage leaf, the grate of one lemon peel, two slices of lemon, one bay leaf, pinch each of ground nutmeg, ground mace, and ground clove. Add the apple to the wine and heat over medium-low temperature. Allow to simmer until the apple is soft and set aside. After one hour, preheat a sauté pan and remove the salmon from the marinade shaking off excess oil. Sauté the salmon, turning one time, until done to taste. For the sauce, bring the wine mixture to a boil whisking to combine the wine and apple. Pass through a fine wire sieve. Season the salmon with salt and ground black pepper to taste and plate over the sauce.

- ➢ For the sauce, combine two tablespoons each of powdered sugar and **FISH SAUCE**, one teaspoon of ground ginger, one-half teaspoon of **VINEGAR**, and one-quarter teaspoon of salt. Peel and remove the core from one apple and dice small adding to sauce. Mince one tablespoon each of parsley, chives, and mint leaves adding to the sauce. Salt and pepper the salmon. Sauté the salmon, turning one time, until done to taste. Plate the salmon spooning sauce over the top.

To fry Carp.
Fried Carp

AFTER having fcaled and drawn them, flit them in two, ftrew them over with Salt ; drudge them well with Flour, and fry them in clarified Butter : When they are fried, you may either ferve them dry, and eat them only with Juice of Orange, or elfe you may prepare a Ragoo of Mufhrooms, the Milts of Carps and other Fifh, and Artichoak Bottoms : Fry fome thin Slices of Bread, and put them into the Sauce, together with fome fliced Onion, and fome Capers, let them boil in it. Difh up your Carp, throw your Ragoo upon it, and let your Garniture be fried Crufts of Bread and fliced Lemon.

> Carp filet
> Salt, as needed
> Flour, as needed
> Butter, clarified, as needed

- *Scale and separate carp into two pieces, season with salt, and dredge in bread flour. Melt **BUTTER** in a sauté pan and fry the filets until brown on both sides. Serve the carp with fresh orange juice or for the ragout: Combine one cup of minced artichoke hearts, one-half cup each of minced* mushrooms and onions. Stir in two tablespoons each of capers, one teaspoon of ground white pepper, one tablespoon of lemon juice, and one-quarter cup of orange juice. Allow to rest while preparing and frying the fish.

> For fried carp: Using a stock pot, add fry oil to one-inch in depth and heat to 350°F. While the oil is heating, prepare breading. For each cup of bread flour used, add one tablespoon of salt and two teaspoons of Old Bay® seasoning. After carp is scaled and separated into two pieces, dredge in the seasoned flour and shake off excess. Dip in the cultured buttermilk. Dredge a second time in the seasoned flour. Fry carp until golden brown on each side.

Southern Fried Catfish

> Add one cup of yellow corn meal to the seasoned flour and use catfish instead of carp. Serve with tartar sauce.

Fish and Chips

> Replace the seasoned flour with a batter by combining one cup of flour, one cup of lager, one-half tablespoon each of salt and granulated sugar, and one teaspoon of baking powder in a mixing bowl whisking until smooth in texture. Dredge the carp [or cod] in flour, shake off excess, and dip in the batter. Fry until golden brown on both sides. Serve with tartar sauce.

Tartar Sauce

> Whisk together one cup of mayonnaise with one-quarter cup of minced **PICKLED CUCUMBERS**.

Another Way to drefs Flounders,
Poached Flounder

HAVING flea'd off the black Skin, and fcored the Fifh over on that Side, with a Knife, lay them on a Difh, and pour on them fome Vinegar, and ftrew good Store of Salt, let them lie for half an Hour : In the mean Time, fet fome Water on the Fire, with a little White Wine, Garlick, and fweet Hcrbs, putting to it the Vinegar and Salt; wherein they lay ; when it boils put in the biggeft Fifh, then the next, till all be in ; when they are boiled take them out and drain them very well, then draw fome fweet Butter thick, and mix with it fome Anchovies shred fmall, which being diffolved in the Butter, pour it on the Fifh, ftrewing a little, fliced Nutmeg, and minced Oranges and Barberries.

Flounder, cleaned and skinned
Vinegar, as needed
Salt, as needed
White wine, as needed
Garlic, as needed
Sweet herbs, as needed
Butter, as needed
Anchovy, as needed

Nutmeg, as needed
Oranges, minced, as needed
Barberries, as needed

- For flounder: Clean and filet the flounder, setting aside. Whisk together one cup of **VINEGAR** with two teaspoons of salt. Add the flounder filets and allow to rest for 30 minutes. Combine one-half cup each of water and **WHITE WINE**, one minced clove of garlic, and three sprigs each of parsley and thyme allowing to simmer over medium-low temperature. Using a food processor, blend together eight tablespoons of soft **BUTTER**, four anchovy fillets, and one-quarter teaspoon of ground nutmeg. Peel and mince one orange and set aside. Add one-quarter cup of dried barberries [substitute dried cranberries] to boiling water to rehydrate them. Once the berries have rehydrated, drain and pat dry. After the fish has marinated for 30 minutes, drain the marinade into the wine and bring to a boil. Reduce the temperature to medium-low adding the fish. When the fish is cooked to taste, remove and plate garnishing with butter, minced orange, and barberries.

Turkey

To stuff a Turkey.

Bread Stuffing

Grate a wheat loaf, one quarter of a pound butter, one quarter of a pound salt pork, finely chopped, 2 eggs, little sweet marjoram, summer savory, parsley and sage, pepper and salt (if the pork be not sufficient,) fill the bird and sew up.

The same will answer for all Wild Fowl.

Water Fowls require onions.

The same ingredients stuff a leg of Veal, fresh Pork or a loin of Veal.

>
> Turkey, cleaned and gutted
> Loaf of bread, grated
> 4 ounces butter
> 4 ounces salt pork, minced
> 2 eggs, beaten
> Parsley, chopped, as needed
> Marjoram, chopped, as needed
> Savory, chopped, as needed
> Sage, chopped, as needed
> Pepper, to taste
> Salt, to taste

➤ For turkey stuffing: Cube one pound of stale **WHITE BREAD** and set aside. Dice small one pound of salt pork, two celery stalks, and one medium onion and combine. Melt four tablespoons of **BUTTER** and whisk in one tablespoon of dried parsley, one teaspoon of ground thyme, one-half teaspoon each of ground sage, salt, and ground black pepper. Whisk in two eggs with one and one-half cups of **CHICKEN STOCK**. Combine with bread and pork. Bake at 350°**F** for 30 minutes.

> Alternate method: replace white bread with **CORN BREAD**.

Vegetables

Cabbages.

Cabbage

ALL forts of cabbages and young fprouts muft have plenty of water allowed them to boil in, and when the flalks become tender, or fall to the bottom, it is a proof of their being fufficiently boiled. Then take them off before they lofe their colour ; but remember always to throw fome falt into your water before you put in your greens. You muft fend your young fprouts to table whole as they come out of the pot ; but many people think cabbage is beft chopped, and put into a faucepan, with a piece of butter, ftirring it about for five or fix minutes, till the butter be all melted, then empty it on a difh, and ferve it up.

- Round headed cabbage first appears in England during the 14TH century.

- For cabbage: Chop one pound of cabbage into bite size pieces about one-inch square. Using a sauce pot, combine the cabbage with four tablespoons of **BUTTER** and two tablespoons of lemon juice. Cook over medium temperature, stirring occasionally, until al dente or wilted. Season with salt and ground black pepper to taste.

Spinach.

Spinach

HAVING picked your fpinach very clean, and wafhed it in five or fix waters, put it into a faucepan that will juft hold it, throw a little falt over it, and cover it clofe. Put in no water, but take care to fhake the pan often. Put your faucepan on a clear and quick fire, and as foon as you find your greens are fhrunk and fallen to the bottom, and the liquor that comes out of them boils up, it is a proof your fpinach is enough. Throw them into a clean fieve to drain, and juft give them a gentle fqueeze. Lay them in a plate, and fend them up with butter in a boat, but never pour any over them.

- Prickly spinach arrived in England during the 14th century; however, it was not until the 16th century that smooth leaf spinach appears.

- For spinach: Using a sauce pot, combine 20 ounces of fresh spinach with four tablespoons of **BUTTER** and two tablespoons of lemon juice. Cook over medium temperature, stirring occasionally, until wilted. Season with salt and ground black pepper to taste.

Spinach.

Creamed Spinach

You may drefs your fpinach, if you choofe, in this manner. Pick and wafh your fpinach well, and put it into a ftew-pan, with a little falt. Cover it clofe, and let it ftew till it be tender. Then throw it into a fieve, drain out all the liquor, and chop it fmall, as much in quantity as a French roll. Add to it half a pint of cream, and feafon it with pepper, falt, and grated nutmeg. Put in a quarter of a pound of butter, and let it ftew over the fire for a quarter of an hour, ftirring it frequently. Cut a French roll into long pieces, about as thick as your finger, and fry them. Poach fix eggs, lay them round on the fpinach, and ftick the pieces of roll in and about the eggs. This will ferve as a fide-difh at a fecund courfe, or for a fupper.

➢ For creamed spinach: Using a sauce pot, melt eight tablespoons of **BUTTER** and whisk in one-half cup each of grated parmesan cheese and heavy cream, and one teaspoon of nutmeg. Allow to simmer, stirring occasionally, until **PARMESAN CHEESE** has melted and is incorporated into the cream. The sauce should be smooth in texture. Stir in 20 ounces fresh spinach.

➢ Alternate method: Add **VERMICELLI**.

Carrots.

Carrots

SCRAPE your carrots very dean, put them in the pot, and when they be enough, take them out, and rub them in a clean cloth. Then flice them into a plate, and pour fome melted butter over them. If they be young fpring carrots, half an hour will boil them fufficiently ; if they be large, they will require an hour ; and old Sandwich carrots will take two hours boiling.

- The English cultivated carrots in America at the settlement of Jamestown.

- For carrots: Slice two pounds of carrots into quarter inch rounds. Using a sauce pot, combine the carrots with enough water to cover them. Bring to a boil and reduce the temperature to medium. Allow to simmer until al dente or fork tender. Using a colander, drain the carrots and sauté them in four tablespoons of melted **BUTTER**. Season with salt to taste.

Candied Carrots

- Using a sauce pot, combine one-quarter cup of brown sugar, four tablespoons of **BUTTER**, and two tablespoons of **RED WINE**. Allow to simmer until the sugar has dissolved. Add the carrots, stirring occasionally, and bring to a hard boil. Allow to boil for two minutes.

Cauliflowers fry'd.

Fried Cauliflower

Take two fine cauliflowers, boil them in milk and water, then leave one whole, and pull the other to pieces ; take half a pound of butter, with two fpoonfuls of water, a little duft of flour, and melt the butter in a ftew-pan ; then put in the whole cauliflower cut in two, and the other pulled to pieces, and fry it till it is of a very light brown. Seafon it with pepper and salt. When it is enough, lay the two halves in the middle, and pour the reft all over.

- Cauliflower appears in England in the late 16TH century.

- For cauliflower: Separate the cauliflower head by pulling it apart into pieces. Using a covered sauce pot, combine the cauliflower, four tablespoons of **BUTTER**, and two tablespoons of water. Allow the cauliflower to cook over medium temperature, stirring occasionally, until al dente or fork tender. Season with salt and ground black pepper to taste.

Broccoli.

Broccoli

CAREFULLY ftrip off all the little branches till you come to the top one, and then with a knife peel off all the hard out fide fkin that is on the ftalks and little branches, and then throw them into water. Have ready a flew-pan of water, throw in a little falt, and when it boils put in your broccoli. When the ftalks be tender, it will be enough. Put a piece of toafted bread, foaked in the water the broccoli was boiled in, at the bottom of your difh, and put, your broccoli on the top of it, the fame way as you treated afparagus, and fend it up to table with butter in a boat.

- Broccoli appears in England during the early 18TH century; however, it was not until the 19th century that broccoli appeared in America.

- For broccoli: Separate two pounds of florets from the stems. Using a covered sauce pot, combine four tablespoons of **BUTTER** with the florets. Cook over medium temperature, stirring occasionally, until al dente or fork tender. Season with salt and ground black pepper to taste.

Green Peas.

Peas

YOU muft not fhell your peas till juft before you want them. Put them into boiling water, with a little falt, and a lump of loaf fugar, and when they begin to dent in the middle, they will be enough. Strain them into a fieve, put a good lump of butter into your difh, and ftir them till the butter be melted. Boil a fprig of mint by it felf, chop it fine, and lay it round the edge of your difh in lumps.

- Native to Europe and Asia, cultivation of the English Pea began in the 17TH century.

> For green peas: Using a sauce pot, melt four tablespoons of **BUTTER** with one tablespoon of granulated sugar. Stir in one tablespoon of fresh minced mint leaves and one pound of fresh peas [substitute frozen peas]. Allow to simmer over medium heat until peas start to shrivel. Season with salt to taste.

Pastas and Potatoes

To make Vermicella,
Vermicelli

Mix yolks of eggs and flour together into a pretty ftiff pafte, fo as you can work it up cleverly, then roll it as thin as it is poffible to roll the pafte. Let it dry in the fun, when it is quite dry, with a very fharp knife cut it as thin as poffible, and keep it in a dry place. It will run up like little worms, as vermicella does; though the beft way is to run it through a coarfe fieve, whilft the pafte is foft. If you want fome to be made in hafte, dry it by the fire, and cut it fmall. It will dry by the fire in a quarter of an hour.

This far exceeds what comes from abroad; being frefher;

> 4 large eggs, beaten
> 2 cups bread flour

- "Let it dry in the sun" is preserving the pasta by allowing the dough to dry (dehydrate) until hard and the hot sun will quickly dry the pasta without mold devoloping. Store in an airtight container. The recipe also suggests "run" or push the dough through a coarse sieve, an alternate method in lieu of drying the dough "in the sun", which suggests the dough is moist and pliable. Prior to the 18TH century, Germans were already pressing dough through a coarse sieve creating little dumplings or Spätzle and Italians were making macaroni and vermicelli along with lasagna and ravioli. It's plausible that the recipe is explaining how the writer was taught to make both Spätzle and Vermicelli.

Pasta Dough

❖ *For pasta dough:* Using a medium sized mixing bowl, whisk four eggs and slowly incorporate two cups of bread flour by adding small amounts at a time. Once the flour and eggs are incorporated, use your hands to form a small ball and knead the dough, flouring your hands as necessary to keep the dough from sticking to your hands, until the dough is firm and elastic, about 10 minutes. Wrap the dough in plastic wrap and allow to rest for 30 minutes. Divide the dough into four equal portions. Lightly flour your work area and roll the dough out with a rolling pin as thin as possible. If you are using a pasta roller, start at dial setting one and work upward to five for **MACCHERONCINI** or seven for **VERMICELLI**.

Vermicella.
Vermicelli

➢ Make **PASTA DOUGH** cutting it into thin pieces about five inches in length or if you are using a pasta cutter, use the angel hair pasta attachment.

➢ Alternate method: Purchase prepackaged angel hair pasta.

Maccaroni aka Pipe-Maccaroni.

Maccheroncini

> Make **PASTA DOUGH** cutting it into 1x2 inch pieces. Using a three-sixteenth inch wooden dowel; wrap each piece of dough around the dowel starting at the two-inch width forming a complete circle or use a small macaroni attachment with a pasta maker.

> Alternate method: Purchase prepackaged small smooth ziti pasta noodles.

Maccaroni.

Macaroni & Cheese

HAVING boiled four ounces of maccaroni till it be quite tender, lay it on a fieve to drain, and then put it into a toffing-pan, with about a gill of cream, and a piece of butter rolled in flour. Boil it five minutes, pour it on a plate, lay Parmefan cheefe toafted all over it, and, as it foon grows cold, fend it up on a water-plate.

4 ounces macaroni
5 ounces cream
Butter, as needed,
Flour, as needed
Parmesan cheese, as needed

❖ *Melt* **BUTTER** *in a sauce pot and whisk in bread flour. When the flour starts to bubble, whisk in five ounces of cream and cooked macaroni. Top with* *grated* **PARMESAN CHEESE** *and place under a broiler until the cheese has lightly browned.*

Modern recipes incorporate the cheese into the sauce [flour, butter, cream], topping with bread crumbs, and broiling until the bread is lightly browned.

This recipe ingredients are used to make modern Mornay sauce.

- For macaroni and cheese: Boil four ounces of **MACCHERONCINI** and set aside. Prepare **MORNAY** and stir in the maccheroncini noodles.
- Alternate method: Top with seasoned bread crumbs and place under a broiler until lightly browned.

Potatoes.

Candied Sweet Potatoes

CUT your potatoes into thin dices, as big as a crown-piece, and fry them brown. Lay them in a difh or plate, and pour melted butter, fack, and sugar, over them. Thefe are a pretty corner plate.

Potatoes, as needed
Butter, melted, as needed
Wine, as needed
Sugar, as needed

- Sweet potatoes appeared in English cooking during the 16TH century and were prepared using spices and sugar making puddings [desserts].

- ➢ For candied potatoes: Slice two pounds of sweet potatoes into one-inch pieces. Using a sauce pot, add potato slices with enough water to cover. Bring to a boil. Reduce the temperature to medium and allow to simmer until fork tender and drain. Using a sauce pot, combine one-half cup of brown sugar, three tablespoons of **BUTTER**, one-quarter teaspoon each of ground nutmeg and cinnamon, and one-quarter cup of **RED WINE**. Bring to a hard boil. Continue to boil for one minute. Reduce the temperature to medium and add the potatoes. Allow to simmer for two minutes stirring occasionally.

Sweet Potato Pie

- ➢ Puree the cooked sweet potato slices using a food processor. Measure the puree and put it in a mixing bowl. For every 16 ounces of puree, whisk in two cups of milk, four beaten eggs, one-half cup molasses, one-quarter teaspoon of allspice, and one-half teaspoon of ground ginger. Prepare **PIE DOUGH** rolling to one-eighth inch thick. Line a pie pan with the dough. Pour the filling into the dough and bake at 350°**F** until the center is set.

Potatoes.

Boiled Potatoes

THOUGH greens require plenty of water to be boiled in, potatoes muſt have only a quantity ſufficient to keep the faucepan from burning. Keep them cloſ'e covered, and as foon as the ſkins begin to crack, they will be enough. Having drained out all the water, let them ſtand covered Tor a minute or two. Then peel them, lay them in a plate, and pour fome melted butter over them.

Potatoes, as needed
Water, as needed
Butter, melted, as needed

- White potatoes appeared in Europe in the late 16TH century.

- For boiled potatoes: Peel potatoes and place in a stock pot with enough water to cover. Bring to a boil. Reduce the temperature to medium and allow the potatoes to simmer until fork tender. Drain and serve with melted **BUTTER**.

Potatoes.

Grilled Potatoes

A very good method of doing them is thus: When they be peeled, lay them on a gridiron till they be of a fine brown, and then fend them to table.

Potatoes, as needed

Peeling potatoes before placing them on a heated grill will dry the outer portion of the potato while baking, leaving a hard unappetizing crust.

> For grilled potatoes: Wrap the potatoes in aluminum foil with two tablespoons of water. Bake at 350°F [or place on a grill] until fork tender. Serve with melted **BUTTER**.

> Alternate method: After baking, split the potato down the middle and squeeze the ends to open up the center. Pour melted **BUTTER** over of the potato before serving. Top with **CRÈME FRAÎCHE**, crumbled bacon, or broccoli and **MORNAY** sauce.

Potatoes.

Fried Potatoes

Another method is, put them into a faucepan, with fome good beef dripping, then cover them clofe, and frequently fhake the faucepan to prevent their burning. As foon as they become of a fine brown, and are crifp, take them up in a plate, then put them into another for fear of the fat, put butter into a boat, and ferve them up.

Potatoes, as needed
Beef fat, as needed
Butter, as needed

91

- For fried potatoes: Cut the potatoes into one-quarter inch slices. Sauté in oil until browned, stirring occasionally to prevent the potatoes from burning. Season with salt and ground black pepper to taste.

- Alternate method: Add diced onion to the potatoes.

Country Style Potatoes

- The potatoes are medium diced instead of sliced. Add green bell pepper and onion diced small to the potatoes before sautéing.

- Alternate method: After frying, combine one teaspoon of salt, one-half teaspoon each of ground black pepper, garlic powder, and paprika, and season the potatoes to taste.

scalloped potatoes.

Twice Baked Potatoes

HAVING boiled your potatoes, beat them fine in a bowl, with fome cream, a large piece of butter, and a little falt. Put them into fcollop-fhells, make them fmooth on the top, fcore hem with a knife, and lay thin flices of butter on the top of them. Then put them into a Dutch oven to brown before the fire. This is a pretty little dilh for a light fupper.

Potatoes, as needed
Heavy Cream, as needed
Butter, as needed
Salt, to taste

The definition of scallop:

- a baking dish in the shape of a marine ribbed shell, or
- the edible muscle contained in a marine ribbed shell.
- Early 18TH century scalloped potatoes were mashed potatoes pressed into a scallop baking dish and cooked a second time.

The outside or skin of the potato replaced the scallop baking dish. The potato filling is piped into the skin to resemble the look of the shell.

- The first mention of sliced scalloped potatoes is in the late 18TH century.

The potatoes were, and still are today, cut into thick slices resembling the edible muscle and baked with cream, butter, and salt.

Although many recipes for scalloped potatoes include cheese, scalloped potatoes contain no cheese at all. It is au gratin potatoes that are covered in cheese and baked until browned and do not appear until the early 19TH century.

- For twice baked potatoes: Prepare **GRILLED POTATOES** and slice in one-half lengthwise spooning out the center reserving the skin as a shell. Weigh the scooped potatoes and place them into a bowl. For every one pound of potatoes, add four peeled and crushed garlic cloves, one-half cup of heavy cream, one-quarter cup of grated **PARMESAN CHEESE**, four tablespoons of melted **BUTTER**, and one-half teaspoon of salt. Mash the potatoes thoroughly combining all the ingredients. Pipe the potatoes into the reserved skins and bake at 350°F until brown on top.

- Alternate method: Replace parmesan cheese with three-quarter cup of grated white **CHEDDAR CHEESE**.

Scalloped Potatoes

- Peel and slice the potatoes into one-quarter inch pieces and layer in a buttered baking dish. For every one pound of potatoes, whisk together four peeled and crushed garlic cloves, three-quarter cup of heavy cream, and one-half teaspoon of salt. Pour the cream over the potatoes and bake at 250°F until the potatoes are al dente and cream has thickened and bubbling.

Au Gratin Potatoes

- Prepare **SCALLOPED POTATO**. Remove from oven and top with grated Gruyère cheese. Cover with aluminum foil and allow the cheese to melt.

- Alternate method: Prepare **MORNAY** and whisk in one-half cup of grated Gruyère cheese. Combine with potatoes baking at 250°F until the potatoes are fork tender.

Beans and Rice

To drefs Beans and Bacon.
Ham and Beans

WHEN you drefs Beans and Bacon, boil the Bacon by itfelf and the Beans by themfelves, for the Bacon will fpoil the Colour of the Beans. Always throw fome Salt into the Water, and fomeParfley nicely pick'd. When the Beans are enough (which you will know by their being tender) throw them into a Cullender to drain : Take up the Bacon and skin it throw fomeRafpings of Bread over the Top, and if you have an Iron make it red-hot and hold over it, to brown the Top of the Bacon : If you have not one, let it before the Fire to brown. Lay the Beans in the Difh, and the Bacon in the Middle on the Top, and lend them to Table, with Butter in a Bafon.

Bacon, as needed
Beans, as needed
Water, as needed
Parsley, as needed
Salt, to taste

- The seeds from the Windsor bean [broad bean] are known as fava beans, common in the 18TH century, and found in early recipes until the common bean [kidney bean] became more popular.

- For ham and beans: Place one pound of dried fava beans [substitute lima beans] in a sauce pot with enough water to cover them. Bring to a boil and remove from heat. Allow to soak overnight. Drain the beans using a colander and return them to the pot adding two pounds of salt pork medium diced, eight cups of water, one tablespoon of dried parsley, and one large onion diced small. Bring to a boil. Reduce the temperature to medium-low and allow to simmer until the beans are tender. Season with salt and ground black pepper to taste.
- Alternate method: Use smoked ham hock, approximately two pounds, instead of salt pork.

A Fricafey of Kidney Beans.

Red Beans

Take a quart of the feed, when dry, foak them all night in river water, then boil them on flow fire till quite tender ; take & quarter of a peck of onions, flice them thin, fry them in butter till brown ; then take them out of the butter, and put them in a quart of ftrongdraw'd gravy. Boil them till you may mafh them fine, then put in your beans, and give them a boil or two. Seafon with pepper, falt, and nutmeg.

4 cups seed
4 pounds onion
Butter, as needed
4 cups gravy

Pepper, to taste
Salt, to taste
Nutmeg, to taste

- For red beans: Using a sauce pot, combine one pound of dried kidney beans with four cups of water. Bring to a boil and remove from the heat. Allow to soak overnight. Drain the beans using a colander and return them to the pot adding four cups of **VEAL** or **CHICKEN STOCK**. Bring to a boil. Reduce the temperature to medium and allow to simmer until the beans are tender and stock has reduced one-half. Sauté one large onion diced small with one tablespoon of **BUTTER** until opaque and add to the beans. Season the beans with salt, ground black pepper, and ground nutmeg to taste.

- Alternate method: Omit the nutmeg and add one teaspoon of dried oregano, and one-half teaspoon each of cumin, garlic powder, and paprika.

Red Beans and Rice

- Although red beans and rice did not appear until a century later, it was not uncommon to see red beans [kidney bean] and rice used separately as an ingredient in cooking. For red beans and rice, follow the manufacturer's cooking instructions for preparing white rice. Prepare **HAM AND BEANS** using kidney beans instead of fava beans and adding one teaspoon of dried oregano, one-half teaspoon each of cumin, garlic powder, and paprika. Serve the beans over white rice.

The discussion of Refried Beans

To dress Beans in Ragoo.
Refried Beans

BOIL your Beans, fo that the Skins will flip off; take about a Quart, feafon them with Pepper, Salt, and Nutmeg, then flour them, and have ready fome Butter in a Stew-pan, throw in your Beans, fry them of a fine brown, then drain them from the Fat, and lay them in your Difh Have ready a quarter of a Pound of Butter melted, and half a Pint of the blanched Beans boiled, beat in a Mortar, with a very little Pepper, Salt, and Nutmeg ; then by degrees mix them into the Better, and pour over the other Beans. Garnifh with a boiled and fry'd Bean, and fo on till you fill the Rim of your Difh. They are very good without frying, and only plain Butter melted over them.

4 cups beans
Pepper, to taste
Salt, to taste
Nutmeg, to taste
Flour, as needed
Butter, as needed, plus 4 ounces

Frijoles refritos, or well-cooked [refried] beans, are well known in Latin American cuisine. Eden Foods mentions refried beans being introduced "about 100 years ago in northern Mexico" dating the origin to around 1913.

Erna Fergusson mentions frijoles refritos in her book titled Mexican Cookbook published in 1934.

Kidney beans contain a toxin called lectin that requires boiling or soaking the beans to reduce the level of lectin safe for consumption. It is plausible that refried beans were first made from kidney beans as a result of the required soaking or cooking process to remove the harmful toxin prior to being cooked a second time [refried] in preparation of the dish. The recipe instructions are to "beat in a Mortar" or mash the beans to a puree which is the same process for making frijoles refritos.

➢ For refried beans: Prepare **RED BEANS** adding one teaspoon dried oregano and one-half teaspoon each of cumin, garlic powder, and paprika. Using a food processor, puree the beans adding enough **VEAL** or **CHICKEN STOCK** as necessary to form a medium thick paste.

➢ Alternate method: Use pinto beans instead of red beans.

The discussion of Baked Beans

The small White Bean, is best for winter use, and excellent.

Windsor Beans.

Boil in plenty of water, with salt, and a bunch of parsley. Serve parsley and butter; garnish with chopped parsley. The French parboil them, take off the skins, stew them, and when done pour a rich veal gravy over.

To drefs Windfor Beans.

Baked Beans

Take the feed, boil them till they are tender; then blanch them, and fry them in clarified butter. Melt butter, with a drop of vinegar, and pour over them. Stew them with falt, pepper, and nutmeg. Or you may eat them with butter, fack, fugar, and a little powder of cinnamon.

With the introduction of white beans in Europe during the 15th century, Cassoulet, beans with pork in a casserole, was soon created. The British, during the 100-year wars and occupying France at the time, would have learned how to create this dish returning home to Britain with the recipe and technique. The British settlers arriving to Americas would have brought the recipe with them as they arrived; however, it is also believed the origin of baked beans comes from Native Indians who were baking beans in clay pots with bear fat and maple syrup long before the arrival of settlers to Americas. Remember the rhyme "Pease porridge in the pot nine days old?" The settlers were already familiar with cooking in pots long before reaching the New World substantiating the origins of baked beans coming from Cassoulet. Documented recipes tell you "to take off the skins" of the beans saving the seeds for cooking. The beans [seeds] were then cooked or "stewed" in "gravy" and in some cases included "fugar" [sugar].

Dried beans need water to rehydrate and soften. Since there is not enough moisture in bear fat or maple syrup to rehydrate dried beans, the idea that beans were baked using these ingredients would not be credible; however, the discovery of sap is conceivable. Sap has enough moisture to rehydrate dried beans. If the Native Indians used sap, the beans would rehydrate as they cooked. The sap would then reduce during the cooking process into a sweet syrup. History also suggests Native Americans ate the baked beans using a piece of dehydrated venison as a spoon.

Settlers arriving in the Americas would have used local ingredients to create the recipes they brought with them on their journey. Local ingredients included white or red beans, cured pork, and sap. Sap would later be replaced with brown sugar followed by molasses replacing the brown sugar.

- For baked beans: Using a sauce pot, combine one pound of dried navy beans and four cups of water. Bring to a boil and remove from the heat. Allow to soak overnight. Drain the beans using a colander and add four cups of fresh water. Cook the beans until al dente and drain a second time. Using a covered baking dish, combine the beans, one-half pound of salt pork diced small, one-half cup of maple syrup, one teaspoon of mustard powder, and one-half teaspoon of ground black pepper. Bake at 400°F until the syrup is bubbling.

> Alternate method: Use brown sugar or molasses instead of maple syrup.

> Alternate method: Combine one-quarter cup of apple cider, one-quarter cup of brown sugar, one-quarter cup each of onion and roasted red peppers diced small, two tablespoons each of apple cider vinegar and tomato paste, one tablespoon each of molasses and prepared mustard, one teaspoon each of onion powder, garlic powder, paprika, and ground black pepper with the navy beans. Bake at 400°F until the syrup is bubbling.

French beans.

French Cut Green Beans

STRING your beans, cut them in two, and then acrofs ; but if you wifh to do them in a nice manner, cut them into four, and then acrofs, fo that each bean will then be in eight pieces. Put them into falt and water, and when the pan boils, put them in with a little falt. They will be foon done, which may be known by their becoming tender ; but take care that you do not fuffer them to lofe their fine green colour. Lay them in a plate, and fend them up with butter in a boat.

Beans, as needed
Salt, to taste
Butter, as needed

- During the 16TH century, France was introduced to a small, long, slender green bean grown for the pod and not the seed. This French bean was pickled for preserving along with slicing for everyday fare.

➢ For French cut green beans: Cut French beans by length down the middle twice and then across the center for a total of eight pieces. Boil the beans in water until tender. Drain them using a colander. Sauté the beans in **BUTTER**, seasoning with salt to taste.

Eggs, Butter and Cheese

Cream pancakes.

Omelet

MIX the yolks of two eggs with half a pint of cream, two ounces of fugar, and a little beaten cinnamon, mace, and nutmeg. Rub your pan with lard, and fry them as thin as poffible. Grate fugar over them.

2 egg yolks
1 cup heavy cream
2 ounces sugar
Cinnamon, as needed
Mace, as needed
Nutmeg, as needed
Sugar, as needed

- ❖ *Whisk together two egg yolks, eight ounces of cream, one-quarter cup of brown sugar, cinnamon, mace, and nutmeg. Melt lard in a sauté pan and add the egg mixture, frying until cooked. Plate the omelet and sprinkle with powdered sugar.*

- ➢ For omelet: Whisk together two eggs with one-half cup of cream. Using a six-inch non-stick sauté pan over medium temperature, add two tablespoons of **BUTTER** and allow to melt. Add the egg mixture slowly while stirring with a spatula. This allows the egg to evenly cook [stir only until the egg sets on the bottom and then stop stirring]. Once the egg has set on the bottom and not browned, and the top of the egg is slightly runny, add your favorite ingredients: diced onion, green pepper, sausage, tomato, sliced mushrooms, grated cheese, or diced ham. Start at one side of the omelet and fold over one-third. Fold one-third again.

Note: If you don't feel comfortable with the runny portion of the egg, remove the sauté pan from the heat and flip the omelet over. Continue filling with your favorite ingredients and fold the omelet as above.

Stuffed Eggs.

Deviled Eggs

TAKE a Dozen Eggs, boil them hard, peel them, fplit them in two, and take the Yolks out of them, put them in a Mortar with a Bit of Butter, young Onions, fhred Parfley, Mufhrooms, and a Piece of Crumb of Bread boiled in Milk ; if you have any Flefh of Fifh put fome in it, and feafon it with Salt, Pepper, fweet Herb, and fine Spices. Pound them all well together, and fill the Whites of your Eggs with it, and fmooth them by dipping your Knife in Egg. Then take the Difh you defign to ferve them in, put fome Farce at the Bottom of it, then put your ftuffed Whites of Eggs in Order upon it ; then bread them, and bake them in an Oven, to give them a Colour. When they are done, put a little Sauce of any-thing you think proper, without covering them ; and ferve them hot for a fecund Courfe.

12 eggs, hard boiled
Onion, as needed
Parsley, as needed
Mushrooms, as needed
1 slice bread
Milk, as needed
Fish, as needed
Salt, to taste
Pepper, to taste
Sweet herbs, to taste
Spices, to taste

- ❖ *Take a dozen hard boiled eggs slicing each egg down the middle lengthwise. Remove the yolks and mix them well with **BUTTER**, onion, parsley, mushrooms, one slice of bread boiled in milk. Seasoning with salt, ground black pepper, herbs and spices. Spoon the mixture into the egg whites topping with bread crumbs. Broil the eggs in an oven until crumbs have toasted.*

- Stuffed eggs can be traced back to the Roman civilization where eggs were boiled hard and filled with various ingredients and sauces. The word 'devil' appears in late 18TH century cooking only referring to spiced foods.

It wasn't until a century later that mayonnaise found its way into stuffed or deviled eggs with spicy mustard.

  - ➤ To hard boil eggs: Place eggs into a sauce pot with enough water to cover them. Bring to a boil. Reduce the temperature to medium and allow to simmer for seven minutes. Drain the eggs using a colander and the place them in ice water allowing to cool. When the eggs are cool to the touch, under cold running water, remove the shell from the eggs.

- For deviled eggs: In a bowl, combine six minced large button mushroom tops, two tablespoons of minced onion, two cloves of minced garlic, one teaspoon each of dried thyme, dried parsley, Dijon mustard, **WORCESTERSHIRE SAUCE**, and lemon juice, and three tablespoons of milk. Slice each egg in half lengthwise and remove the yolk. Thoroughly mix together the egg yolks and mushroom mixture. Spoon the mixture back into the egg whites being careful not to tear the whites. Top the eggs with breadcrumbs and place under a broiler until the breadcrumbs are toasted.

- Alternate method: Slice ten eggs in half lengthwise and remove the egg yolk. Whisk together the egg yolks with one-quarter cup of mayonnaise, one teaspoon each of Dijon mustard and **WORCESTERSHIRE SAUCE**, and one and one-half teaspoons of lemon juice. Season the yolks with salt, ground black pepper, and cayenne pepper to taste. Spoon the yolks back into the egg whites being careful not to tear the whites. Garnish the eggs with minced chives, crumbled bacon, or minced **PICKLED CUCUMBERS**.

Sweet Egg Pie.

Quiche

COVER your difh with a good cruft, and then take twelve eggs boiled hard, cut them into flices, and lay them in your pie. Throw half a pound of currants, clean wafhed and picked, all over your eggs. Then beat up four eggs well, mixed with half a pint of white wine, grate in a fmall nutmeg, and make it pretty fweet with fugar. Remember to lay a quarter of a pound of butter between the eggs, then pour in your wine and eggs, and cover your pie. Bake it till the cruft be done, which will be in about half an hour.

> 12 eggs, hard boiled plus 4 eggs
> 8 ounces currants
> 1 cup white wine
> Nutmeg, to taste
> Sugar, as needed
> 4 ounces butter
> Pie crust

- Quiche owes its origins to medieval Germany having a bread crust topped with an egg and cream custard along with bacon. The bread was later replaced with pie dough or puff pastry.
- For quiche: Line a pie pan with **PIE DOUGH**. Whisk together four eggs, two cups of heavy cream, one-half teaspoon of salt, one-quarter teaspoon each of ground black pepper and

ground nutmeg. Mix into the eggs one medium onion diced small, six strips of bacon cooked and crumbled, and one cup of shredded Gruyère cheese. Pour the filling onto the pie dough and bake at 325°F until center of quiche is set and top starts to turn light brown.

- Alternate method: Replace Gruyère with Swiss cheese.
- Alternate method: Add three cups of fresh spinach.

The difference between a quiche and frittata is the use of pie dough crust for quiche where a frittata has no crust.

The discussion of Cheese

- During the 18th century, cheese makers would wrap cheese in inexpensive fabric coating with lard. This would add a protective seal and aid in reducing moisture loss. In earlier periods, the cheese would have been salted creating a hard rind sealing and protecting the cheese during aging.
- Dunlop cheese dates back to the 16th century. The recipe used whole milk replacing skimmed milk used previously in cheese making. It is suggested that Cheddar cheese, named after the large village of Cheddar in Somerset England, owes its origins to this cheese.

- Cheshire cheese, using milk from Cheshire cows, was traded as early as the 17TH century and was the only cheese purchased by the Royal Navy beginning in 1739.

- In 1758, the Royal Navy ordered all ships to be stocked with Gloucester cheese, made of milk from Gloucester cows.

- The caves in which this cheese is aged contain mold. Penicillium Roqueforti is found in the local caves of Southern France where Roquefort cheese is produced and aged.

- Dating back to the 13TH century, Parmigiano-Reggiano is the most popular cheese of Italy. If this cheese is produced outside of the country, it is referred to as Parmesan.

- This cheese was in existence back in 774 at the time of Charles the Great. Brie de Meaux [Brie] is often called the King of Cheese.

Although pasteurizing was discovered in 1856, pasteurizing milk did not occur until 1882. Fresh unpasteurized milk has natural bacteria that are killed during pasteurization which makes it unsuitable to make cheese without adding a starter culture.

    i. When recreating recipes, the use of buttermilk and yogurt will be used for a live culture in the recipes.

ii. Ultra-pasteurized milk or cream is not used for cheese making because the milk fats are no longer stable from the high temperature.

iii. Allow fresh bread to rest in a cool area to promote mold to grow [blue mold or Penicillium Roqueforti]. After the mold has developed and the bread is dry, crush the bread to a fine powder and add one teaspoon per gallon of milk to create Roquefort or blue cheese.

iv. Allow citrus peels to rest in a cool area to promote the growth of mold [white mold]. Use one teaspoon of this mold per gallon of milk to create Brie.

v. Rennet is commonly used to coagulate the milk or cream; however, since rennet is not readily available in a grocery store, vinegar, or lemon juice [acidic] can be used in place of rennet.

vi. Since types of molds can be dangerous to consume, the recipes use purchased pencillium mold. Purchased rennet can be used in place of acid [lemon juice or vinegar].

Cream cheefe.

Cream Cheese

TO five quarts of gafterings put one large fpoonful of fteep, and break it down light. Then put it upon a cloth on a fieve bottom, and let it run till dry. Break it, cut and turn it in a clean cloth. Then put it into the fieve again, and put on it a two-pound weight, fprinkle a little falt on it, and let it ftand all night. Then lay it on a board to dry, and when it be dry, lay a few ftrawberry leaves on it, and ripen it between two pewter difhes in a warm plate. Turn it, and put on frefh leaves every day.

5 quarts fresh milk
1 tablespoon rennet
Salt, as needed
Strawberry leaves, as needed

> For cream cheese: Using a stock pot, combine 112 ounces of whole milk and 16 ounces of heavy cream. Heat the milk while gently stirring to 90°F. Once the milk has reached 90°F, stir in four ounces of buttermilk and one-quarter cup lemon juice or vinegar. Continue to slowly stir for one minute. Cover the pot with a towel and allow to rest for 12 hours. At this point you should see a large curd in the middle of the pot surrounded by whey. Line a colander with fine weave cheesecloth [butter muslin] and drain the curds for two hours. Gently mix one teaspoon of non-iodized salt into the curds. Allow the curds to drain for 10 hours. Using a food processor, whip the cheese into a cream. Refrigerate.

Cheddar Cheese

Cheddar, Cheshire, Gloucester

> For Cheddar cheese: Place 256 ounces of whole milk in a large stock pot. Heat the milk to 86°F while gently stirring. Stir in eight ounces of plain unflavored Greek yogurt and continue to slowly stir for one minute. Remove from heat and allow to rest undisturbed for 90 minutes. After 90 minutes, add one-half cup lemon juice or vinegar and stir for one minute. Allow to rest undisturbed for 45 minutes. After 45 minutes, you should see a large curd in the middle of the pot surrounded by whey. Using a long knife, slice the curds into one-inch pieces. While slowly and gently stirring the curds, bring the temperature back to 86°F. Raise the temperature two degrees every five minutes until the temperature reaches 100°F. Maintain 100°F while slowly and gently stirring the curds for 30 minutes. Using a colander, drain the curds. Using a stock pot large enough to hold the colander on the rim of the pot, fill the pot one-quarter full of water and bring the water temperature to 125°F. Set the colander on the rim of the pot to keep the curds warm. Turn the curds every 15 minutes for two hours. After two hours, evenly mix in one and one-half teaspoons of non-iodized salt per pound of cheese curds. Once the curds are salted, they are ready to be pressed into a mold. After three days, remove the curd from the mold and coat with cheese wax.

> Alternate method: Wrap in fine cheesecloth or butter muslin and evenly coat with lard [substitute butter].

Allow the cheese to age for six months.

Blue cheese

Roquefort

> For blue cheese: Place 256 ounces of whole milk in a large stock pot. Heat the milk to 80°F while gently stirring. Remove the pot from the heat and stir in Penicillium Roqueforti, [purchased following the manufacturer's instructions] generally one-eighth teaspoon for two gallons of milk. Slowly stir for one minute. Allow the milk to rest undisturbed for 90 minutes. After 90 minutes, add one-half cup lemon juice or vinegar and stir for one minute. Allow the milk to rest undisturbed for 90 minutes. After 90 minutes, you should see a large curd in the middle of the pot surrounded by whey. Using a long knife, slice the curd into one-inch pieces. While slowly and gently stirring the curds, bring the temperature back to 80°F. Maintain 80°F while slowly and gently stirring the curds for 30 minutes. Using a colander, drain the curds. The curds are ready to be placed in a mold. After three days, remove the curd from the mold and evenly salt all sides of the curd using one and one-half teaspoons of non-iodized salt per pound of cheese curds. Allow the cheese to age for five months.

Parmesan cheese

Parmigiano-Reggiano

> For parmesan cheese: Place 256 ounces of whole milk in a large stock pot. Heat the milk to 86°F while gently stirring. Remove the pot from the heat and stir in eight ounces of plain unflavored Greek yogurt. Slowly stir for one minute. Allow the milk to rest undisturbed for 90 minutes. After 90 minutes, add one-half cup lemon juice or vinegar and stir for one minute. Allow the milk to rest undisturbed for 45 minutes. After 45 minutes, you should see a large curd in the middle of the pot surrounded by whey. Whisk the curds into one-quarter inch pieces. While slowly and gently stirring the curds, bring the temperature back to 86°F. Raise the temperature two degrees every five minutes until the temperature reaches 120°F. Maintain 120°F while slowly and gently stirring the curds for 30 minutes. Using a colander, drain the curds. The curds are ready to be placed in a mold. After three days, remove the curd from the mold. Make a salt water brine by dissolving 20 ounces of canning and pickling salt in 64 ounces of hot water. The brine should be at room temperature for the next step. For every pound of cheese, place the block of curd into the brine for six hours. Turn the cheese over in one-half the amount of brining time required. Remove the block of curd from the brine and allow aging for 10 months.

Brie

Brie

> For Brie: Using a stock pot, combine 112 ounces of whole milk and 16 ounces of heavy cream. Heat the milk to 86°F while gently stirring. When the milk reaches 86°F, stir in eight ounces of buttermilk and Penicillium Candidum [purchased following the manufacturer's instructions] generally one-eighth of one teaspoon for two gallons of milk. Slowly stir for one minute. Maintaining 86°F, allow the milk to rest undisturbed for 90 minutes. After 90 minutes, add one-half cup lemon juice or vinegar and stir for one minute. Remove the pot from the heat and allow to rest undisturbed for 45 minutes. After 45 minutes, you should see a large curd in the middle of the pot surrounded by whey. The curd is ready to be placed in a mold. Make sure the whey is draining away from the curd when in the mold. Carefully turn the mold over every two hours for 12 hours. After the whey has drained from the curd, remove the curd from the mold and evenly apply a light coat of non-iodized salt. Allow to rest for another 24 hours. Apply a second light coat of non-iodized salt and allow to rest for another 24 hours. Allow the cheese to age six weeks.

Rennet can be purchased in various forms: tablet, liquid, or vegetarian, to use in place of the acid in the recipes.

Butter

Butter

- For butter: In a mixing bowl, combine two cups of heavy cream and one-quarter teaspoon of non-iodized salt. Whisk the cream until it turns solid. Spoon the butter onto a sieve draining off the excess whey. Originally, the whey would have been used for making cheese because it still had active bacteria; however, during the process of pasteurizing, healthy bacterium is killed so this whey is of no value and is discarded. Refrigerate.

Sour Cream

Crème Fraîche

- For Crème Fraîche: Combine two cups of heavy cream and two tablespoons of buttermilk in a jar and cover with a lid. Shake the jar thoroughly to mix the cream and buttermilk. Shake the jar two times per day until the cream sets or curdles. The cream should be thick at this time. Refrigerate.

Bread

To make White Bread in the London Manner

White Bread

PUT a bufhel of the fineft well-dressed flour in at one end of the kneeding-trough. Then take a gallon of water, which Bakers call liquor, and fome yeft. Stir it into the liquor till it looks of a good brown colour, and begins to curdle. Strain and mix it with your flour till it be about the thicknefs of a feed-cake, then cover it with the lid of the trough, and let it ftand three hours. As foon as you fee it begin to fall, take a gallon more liquor, weigh three quarters of a pound of falt, and with your hand mix it well with the water. Strain it, and with this liquor make your dough of a moderate thicknefs, fit to make up into loaves. Then coven it again with the lid, and let it fland three hours more. In the mean time put your wood into the oven, which will require two hours heating. Then clear the oven, and begin to make your bread ; put it in, clofe up the oven, and three hours will bake it. When once the bread be put in, you muft not open the oven till the bread be baked; and take care in fummer that your water be milk warm, and in winter as hot as your finger will bear. All flour does not require the fame quantity of water; but that experience will teach you in two or three times making.

Bushel of flour
Water, as needed
Yeast, as needed
Salt, as needed

- For white bread: In a mixing bowl, combine one and one-half cups of bread flour and one cup of warm water mixed with one-half teaspoon of active dry yeast. Whisk them together forming a thick batter and allow to rest for three hours. After three hours, add four cups of bread flour and one cup of warm water mixed with one and three-quarter teaspoons of active yeast. Stir together forming a dough ball. Place the dough in a lightly oiled bowl and cover letting the dough rise until doubled in size. Preheat an oven to 350°F. Knead the dough for six minutes. Separate it into two round loaves. Allow the dough to rise until doubled in size. Bake the bread until golden to light brown.

- For white bread, combine two and one-half teaspoons active dry yeast with 12 ounces of warm water and three tablespoons of olive oil. Whisk together three and one-half cups of bread flour with two teaspoons of salt and one teaspoon of granulated sugar. Combine the water and flour mixtures forming a ball. Knead the dough for six minutes. Cover and allow to rest (proof) until double in size. Knead the dough for two minutes. Divide the dough into two equal portions. Form a ball with each portion of dough. Cover and allow to rest (proof) until double in size. Bake at 350°F until a hard crust forms on the outside of the bread.

> Alternate method: Allow the dough (2ND proofing) to rise in a loaf pan prior to baking.

To make Muffings and Oat-Cakes.

Dinner Roll and English muffin

TO a Bufhel of Hertfordfhire white Flour, take a Pint and half of good Ale-yeaft, from pale Malt if you can get it, becaufe it is whiteft; let the Yeaft lie in Water all Night, the next Day pour off the Water clear, make two Gallons of Water juft Milk warm, not to fcald your Yeaft, and two Ounces of Salt, mix your Water, Yeaft and Salt well together for about a quarter of an Hour, then ftrain it, and mix up your Dough as light as poffible, and let it lie in your Trough an Hour to rife, then with your Hand roll it, and pull it into little Pieces about as big as a large Walnut, roll them with your Hand like a Ball, lay them on your Table, and as faft as you do them lay a Piece of Flannel over them, and before to keep your Dough cover'd with Flannel ; when you have rolled out all your Dough, begin to bake the firft, and by that Time they will be fpread out in the right Form lay them on your Iron, as one Side begins to change Colour turn the other, and take great Care they don't burn, or be too much difcolour'd ; but that you will be a Judge off in two or three Makings. Take Care the middle of the Iron is not too hot, as it will be, but then you may put a Brick-bat or two in the middle of the Fire to flacken the Heat. The Thing you bake on muft be made thus. Build a Place juft as if you was going to fet a Copper, and in the Stead of a Copper a Piece of Iron all over the Top fix'd in Form, juft the fame as the Bottom of an Iron Pot, and make your Fire underneath with Coal as in a Copper; obferve, Muffings are made the fame Way, only this, when you pull them to Pieces roll them in a good deal of Flour, and with a Rolling-pin roll them thin, cover them with a Piece of Flannel, and they will rife to a proper Thicknefs; and if you find them too big or too little, you muft roll Dough accordingly, tbefe muft not be the leaft difcolour'd. And when you eat them, toaft them with a Fork crifp on both Sides, then with your Hand pull them open, and they will be like a Honey-Comb ; lay in as much Butter as you intend to ufe, then clap them together again, and fet it by the Fire, when you think the Butter is melted turn them, that both Sides may be butter'd alike, but don't touch them with a Knife, either to fpread or cut them open, if you do they will be as heavy as Lead, only when they are quite butter'd and done, you may cut them acrofs with a Knife.

Bushel of flour
24 ounces of ale yeast
2 gallons of milk
2 ounces of salt

Dinner Roll

➢ Prepare **WHITE BREAD** and separate into equal portions the size of a large walnut rolling into round balls. Lightly oil a baking sheet and equally distribute the rolls onto the sheet. Allow the rolls to rise until doubled in size. Bake the dinner rolls at 350°F until light brown in color.

English Muffin

➢ Prepare **DINNER ROLL** and flatten to one-quarter inch thickness. Lightly oil a baking sheet and distribute the muffins equally on the sheet. Allow the muffins to rise until doubled in size. Bake the muffins at 350°F until light brown in color.

Naples Bifcuit.
Savoiardi

SIFT a pound of fine fugar, and put to it three quarters of the fineft flower which can be got, it muft be fifted three times ; then add fix eggs well beat, and a fpoonful of rofe water ; when the oven is almoft hot, make them, but take care they are not made up too wet.

To make French Bifcuits

French Biscuits

Having a pair of clean fcales ready, in one fcale put three new laid eggs, in the other fcale put as much dried flour, an equal weight with the eggs, take out the flour, and as much fine powdered fugar ; firft beat the whites of the eggs up well with a wifk till they are of a fine froth, then whip in half an ounce of candied lemon-peel cut very thin and fine, and beat well; then by degrees whip in the flour and fugar, then flip in the yolks, and with a fpoon temper it well together, then fhape your bifcuits on fine white paper with your fpoon, and throw powdered fugar over them. Bake them in a moderate oven, not to hot, giving them a fine colour on the top. When they are baked, with fine knife cut them off from the paper, and lay them in boxes for ufe.

Eggs, as needed
Flour, as needed
Powdered, as needed
Lemon-peel, as needed

- These cookies or biscuits date back to early 18TH century France and Italy.
- For the batter: Separate two large eggs. Whisk the egg whites to a stiff peak and whisk in two tablespoons of minced lemon candy peel. Whip

the egg yolks until smooth. Sift two and one-half ounces of bread flour with two and one-half ounces of powdered sugar. Slowly fold the flour mixture and yolks into the egg whites being careful not to over mix. When ingredients are thoroughly combined, spoon the batter onto a baking sheet pan lined with parchment paper and bake at 300°F until dry and crisp. Remove and allow to cool.

➢ For French biscuits aka ladyfingers: Form the **BATTER** into one-inch by four-inch lines.

➢ For savoiardi aka vanilla wafers: Spoon the **BATTER** into two-inch round circles.

➢ Alternate method: Add two teaspoons of vanilla extract.

Depending on the country and region, you could be preparing biscotti, French biscuit, or savoiardi. All three share the same ingredients; however, each has its own shape and size.

Pastry Dough

Puff Paftes for Tarts.

Pie Dough

No. 3. To any quantity of flour, rub in three fourths of it's weight of butter, (twelve eggs to a peck) rub in one third or half, and roll in the rest.

> Flour, as needed
> Butter, as needed
> Eggs, as needed

❖ *For pie dough: In a mixing bowl, combine 13-1/3 ounces of pastry flour and nine ounces of* **BUTTER**. *Mix by hand, until the flour forms a coarse crumb. Whisk three eggs in a small bowl and add two and one-half of the eggs to the flour thoroughly mixing and forming a ball. On a well-floured board, roll the dough to a one-quarter inch thick square. With the remaining beaten egg, brush the egg on one-half of the dough, folding in the middle, and rolling out until double in size keeping a square. Use enough flour to keep dough from sticking to your board and roller. Repeat the steps until egg is gone. Divide the dough into four equal portions. Roll each portion of dough into a round circle one-eighth inch thick. The recipe should make two eight-inch pie shells each with a pie dough cover.*

➢ Alternate method: In a mixing bowl, combine 13-1/3 ounces of pastry flour and nine ounces of **BUTTER**. Mix by hand until the flour forms a coarse crumb. Add two ounces of ice water to the flour thoroughly mixing and forming a ball. If necessary, add enough extra ice water to make the dough firm but not sticky. Divide the dough into four equal portions. Use enough flour to keep dough from sticking to your board and roller. Roll each portion of dough into a round circle one-eighth inch thick. The recipe should make two eight-inch pie shells each with a pie dough cover.

➢ Alternate method: Purchase packaged pie dough at your local grocery store.

Royal Paste.
Puff Pastry

No. 9. Rub half a pound of butter into one pound of flour, four whites beat to a foam, add two yolks, two ounces of fine sugar; roll often, rubbing one third, and rolling two thirds of the butter is best; excellent for tarts and apple cakes.

8 ounces butter
16 ounces flour
4 egg whites
2 egg yolks
2 ounces sugar

- ❖ Separate four eggs into two bowls:
  - Bowl one, four egg whites,
  - Bowl two, two egg yolks.

  Whisk the egg whites to a stiff peak. Whisk the yolks with two ounces of granulated sugar. In a mixing bowl, combine 16 ounces of bread flour with three ounces of **BUTTER**. *Mix by hand until the flour forms a coarse crumb. Combine the flour, egg whites, and egg yolks forming a stiff ball. On a well-floured board, roll dough to one-half inch thick square. Take one-fifth of the remaining butter and brush on one-half of the dough. Fold the dough in the middle rolling out until double in size keeping square. Use enough flour to keep dough from sticking to your board and roller. Repeat steps until the butter is gone.*

- ➤ For puff pastry: Using a mixing bowl, combine two cups of bread flour with one cup of water mixing until the flour forms a stiff ball. On a well-floured board, roll the dough into a rectangle one-half inch thick. Pound eight ounces of **BUTTER** into a rectangle two-thirds the size of the dough. Place the butter on two-thirds of the dough, and the unbuttered portion of the dough is folded over. One-half of the buttered portion is folded on top of the current fold creating three equal layers and rolled to one-half inch thick. The dough is chilled before folding the dough into another three layers and rolled out to one-half inch thick. This process is repeated another three times.

➤ Alternate method: Purchase packaged puff pastry sheets at your local grocery store.

Puddings and Syllabubs

A Bread Pudding.
Bread Pudding

One pound soft bread or biscuit soaked in one quart milk, run thro' a sieve or cullender, add 7 eggs, three quarters of a pound sugar, one quarter of a pound butter, nutmeg or cinnamon, one gill rose-water, one pound stoned raisins, half pint cream, bake three quarters of an hour, middling oven.

> 16 ounces bread or biscuit
> 32 ounces of milk
> 7 eggs
> 12 ounces of sugar
> 4 ounces of butter
> Nutmeg or cinnamon, to taste
> 5 ounces of rose water
> 16 ounces of raisins
> 1 cup heavy cream

> For bread pudding: Soak eight ounces of **WHITE BREAD, FRENCH BISCUIT** or **SAVOIARDI** in three-quarter cup of milk until soft and press through a colander. Whisk together four eggs, three-quarter cup of brown sugar, two ounces of grated **BUTTER**, one and one-half teaspoons each of grated nutmeg and cinnamon, one-half cup plus two tablespoons of **ROSE WATER**, one cup of raisins, and one-half cup of heavy cream.

Combine the egg mixture and bread. Butter a baking dish and spoon in the pudding mixture. Bake at 350°F, on the middle rack in the oven, until center is set.

> Alternate method: Dice **WHITE BREAD** into one-inch cubes. Using a mixing bowl, whisk the rest of the ingredients. Stir in the bread and allow to soak until saturated. Place the bread cubes in a baking dish; pour the remaining milk mixture over the bread and continue with the baking process.

A Rice Pudding.
Rice Pudding

One quarter of a pound rice, a stick of cinnamon, to a quart of milk (stirred often to keep from burning) and boil quick, cool and add half a nutmeg, 4 spoons rose-water, 8 eggs; butter or puff paste a dish and pour the above composition into it, and bake one and half hour.

A Rice Pudding.
Rice Pudding

No. 6. Put 6 ounces rice into water, or milk and water, let swell or soak tender, then boil gently, stirring in a little butter, when cool stir in a quart cream, 6 or 8 eggs well beaten, and add cinnamon nutmeg, and sugar to your taste, bake.

6 ounces of rice
Water or milk, as needed
Butter, as needed
6 to 8 eggs, beaten
Cinnamon, to taste
Nutmeg, to taste
Sugar, to taste

- For the filling: Weigh six ounces of dry rice and follow the manufacturer's directions for cooking. Add one tablespoon of **BUTTER** and stir until the butter is melted. Allow to cool to room temperature. Whisk together four cups of heavy cream, eight beaten eggs, one-quarter cup of brown sugar, one and one-half teaspoons of ground cinnamon, and one and one-quarter teaspoons of ground nutmeg. Combine the cream mixture and rice.

- For frittata: Butter a pie pan and pour in the filling. Bake at 350°F until the center has set, about 40 minutes.

- For quiche: Line a pie pan with pie dough and par-bake. Pour in the filling. Bake at 350°F until the center has set and the crust is golden brown, about 40 minutes.

I found that baking the pie at a high temperature scrambled the eggs; so, to prevent the eggs from scrambling, scald the milk and slowly whisk it into the eggs.

A Cream Almond Pudding.

English Almond Custard

Boil gently a little mace and half a nutmeg (grated) in a quart cream; when cool, beat 8 yolks and 3 whites, strain and mix with one spoon flour one quarter of a pound almonds; settled, add one spoon rose-water, and by degrees the cold cream and beat well together; wet a thick cloth and flour it, and pour in the pudding, boil hard half an hour, take out, pour over it melted butter and sugar.

> 32 ounces heavy cream
> Mace, to taste
> 1/2 grated nutmeg
> 8 egg yolks
> 3 egg whites
> 1 tablespoon flour
> 4 ounces almonds
> 1 tablespoon rose water

Unlike American puddings, English pudding simply refers to a dessert.

❖ *For English almond custard: Whisk together eight egg yolks, three egg whites, and one tablespoon of pastry flour. Whisk in four cups of boiled heavy cream, one-half cup of almonds (ground), one tablespoon of* **ROSE WATER**, *ground mace, and one-half teaspoon of ground nutmeg. Fill a stock pot one-half full of water and bring to a boil. Reduce the temperature to medium-high. Wet a piece of cloth, rub with bread flour, and shake off the* *excess. Using a bowl, press the cloth down the inside creating a well for the filling. Pour the filling into the well and bring the edges of the cloth together tying closed with baker's twine. Gently set the cloth inside the water and allow to boil for 30 minutes. To prepare the sauce, melt equal portions of brown sugar and* **BUTTER** *in a sauce pot and bring to a hard boil. After 30 minutes, remove the cloth, untie, and cut the pudding in half. Plate the pudding topped with the sauce.*

➢ Alternate method: Bring 20 ounces of milk to a boil and remove from heat. Whisk together four eggs, four ounces of granulated sugar, two teaspoons of vanilla extract, two teaspoons of pastry flour, one-quarter teaspoon each of ground nutmeg and ground mace, and two tablespoons of ground almonds. While whisking the egg mixture, slowly add the hot milk tempering the eggs. Pour the pudding into buttered ramekins and set them inside a roasting pan. Pour enough water in the pan to cover halfway up the side of the ramekins. Using medium-high temperature, heat the water until it starts to steam and then place the lid on the pan. Reduce the temperature to medium-low and allow to steam for 30 minutes. Do not allow the water to boil.

➢ Alternate method: Using a saucepan, combine four tablespoons of butter, one-quarter cup of brown sugar, two tablespoons of water, and one-half teaspoon of vanilla extract. Slowly stir the ingredients bringing to a boil. Continue to stir and allow to boil for one minute. Remove from heat and allow to cool. Serve over pudding.

An Apple Pudding Dumplin.
Apple Dumpling

Put into paste, quartered apples, lye in a cloth and boil two hours, serve with sweet sauce.

Paste, as needed
Apples, as needed
Sweet sauce, as needed

The misconception of this recipe is the use of the word paste. The paste in the recipe is not a smooth, sticky, flour and water mixture applied to the outside of the apple. The paste refers to puff paste or pie dough.

❖ *For apple dumplings: Peel and cut Granny Smith apples into quarters removing the core and seeds. Prepare* **PIE DOUGH** *rolling to one-eighth inch thick and cutting into about ten-inch circles. In the center of the dough, place one apple cut into quarters and brush the outside rim of the dough with water. Bring the outside of the dough together forming a ball. Place the ball in the center of a twelve-inch square piece of cheesecloth and bring the ends of the cheesecloth together tying closed with baker's twine. Fill a stock pot one-half full of water and bring to a boil. Reduce the temperature to medium-high and place the dumplings into the water. Allow the dumplings to boil for 30 minutes. Remove and discard the cheesecloth. For the sweet sauce, combine* two cups of each of brown sugar and water, eight tablespoons of **BUTTER**, and one teaspoon of ground cinnamon in a sauce pot. Bring to a hard boil. Plate the dumplings topped with the sauce.

> Alternate method: Prepare **FRIED APPLES** and **PIE DOUGH**. Roll the dough to one-eighth inch thick and cut into eight-inch circles. In the center of the dough, place one apple cut into quarters and brush the outside rim of the dough with water. Bring the outside of the dough together forming a ball. Pour the **SWEET SAUCE** into a baking pan and place the dumplings into the pan with the sauce. Bake at 350°F until the dough is golden brown in color. Plate the dumplings and spoon sauce over top.

Apple Pudding.

English Apple tart

One pound apple sifted, one pound sugar, 9 eggs, one quarter of a pound butter, one quart sweet cream, one gill rose-water, a cinnamon, a green lemon peal grated (if sweet apples,) add the juice of half a lemon, put on to paste No. 7. Currants, raisins and citron some add, but good without them.

16 ounces apples
16 ounces sugar
9 eggs
4 ounces butter
32 ounces heavy cream

5 ounces rose water
Cinnamon, as needed
Peel of 1 lime, grated
Juice of 1/2 lemon
Paste, as needed

> For English apple tart: Simmer 16 ounces of Granny Smith apples [peeled, quartered, and core removed] with two cups of brown sugar and four cups of heavy cream until soft. Using a blender, puree the apples. Whisk nine eggs in a bowl. While briskly whisking the eggs, temper them by slowly adding the pureed apples. Whisk in eight tablespoons of melted **BUTTER**, one teaspoon of ground cinnamon, five ounces of **ROSE WATER**, the grated peel of one lime and one tablespoon of lemon juice. Prepare **PIE DOUGH** rolling to one-eighth inch thick and line a tart pan with the dough. Pour the apple filling onto the dough and bake at 350°F until center is set.

Orange Pudding.

English Orange Tart

Put sixteen yolks with half a pound butter melted, grate in the rinds of two Seville oranges, beat in half pound of fine Sugar, add two spoons orange water, two of rose-water, one gill of wine, half pint cream, two naples biscuit or the crumbs of a fine loaf, or roll soaked in cream, mix all together, put it into rich puff-

paste, which let be double round the edges of the dish; bake like a custard.

A Lemon Pudding.

English Lemon Tart

1. Grate the yellow of the peals of three lemons, then take two whole lemons, roll under your hand on the table till soft, taking care not to burst them, cut and squeeze them into the grated peals.

2. Take ten ounces soft wheat bread, and put a pint of scalded white wine thereto, let soak and put to No. 1.

3. Beat four whites and eight yolks, and put to above, adding three quarters of a pound of melted butter, which let be very fresh and good) one pound fine sugar, beat all together till thorougly mixed.

4. Lay paste No. 7 or 9 on a dish, plate or saucers, and fill with above composition.

5. Bake near 1 hour, and when baked--stick on pieces of paste, cut with a jagging iron or a doughspur to your fancy, baked lightly on a floured paper; garnished thus, they may be served hot or cold.

> Whisk together four eggs, four ounces of granulated sugar, and two teaspoons of pastry flour. Bring 20 ounces of milk to a boil. While

whisking the egg mixture, slowly add the hot milk tempering the eggs. Prepare puff pastry rolling to one-eighth inch thick and docking the dough by using a fork and poking little holes all over the dough. Line a tart pan with the dough. Preheat an oven to 300°F. Prebake the dough until it starts to brown, about 10 minutes. Pour the filling onto the dough and bake at 300°F until dough is light brown and the filling has set, about one hour. Remove and allow to cool.

- For English lemon tart: Whisk in one-half cup lemon juice and the grated peel of two lemons.

- For English orange tart: Whisk in one-half cup of orange juice concentrate and the grated peel of two oranges.

The discussion of Syllabub and Whipped Cream

To make Whipt Cream.

Take a quart of thick cream, and the whites of eight eggs beat well, with half a pint of fack ; mix it together, and fweeten it to your tafle with double-refined fugar. You may perfume it, if you pleafe, with a little mufk or amber-greafe tied in a rag, and fteeped a little in the cream, whip it up with a wifk, and fome lemon-peel tied

in the middle of the wifk ; take the froth with a fpoon, and lay it in your glaffes or bafons. This does well over a fine tart

To make Whipt Syllabubs.

Take a quart of thick cream, and half a pint of fack, the juice of two Seville oranges or lemons, grate in the peel of two, lemons, half a pound of double-refined fugar, pour it into a broad earthen pan, and wifk it well; but firft fweeten fome red wine or fack, and fill your glaffes as full as you chufe ; then as the, froth rifes take it off with a fpoon; lay it carefully into your glaffes till they are as full as they will hold. Don't make thefe long before you ufe them. Many ufe cyder fweetened or any wine you pleal'e, or lemon, or orange whey made thus fqueeze the juice of a lemon or orange into a quarter of a pint of milk, when the curd is hard, pour the whey clear off, and fweeten it to your palate. You may colour fome with juice of fpinach, fome with faffron, and fome with cochineal, juft as you fancy,

To make everlafting Syllabubs,

Take five half pints of thick cream, half a pint Rhenifh, half a pint of fack and the juice of two large Seville oranges ; grate in juft the yellow rhind of three lemons, and a pound of double-refined fugar well beat and lifted ; mix all together with a fpoonful of orange-flower water, beat it well together with a wifk half an hour, then with a fpoon fill your glades. Thefe will keep above a week, and are better made the day before. The beft way to whip fyllabub is, have a fine large chocolate mill, which you muft keep on purpofe, and a large deep bowl to mill them in. It is both quicker done, and the froth ftronger. For the thin that is left at the bottom, have ready fome calf foot jelly boiled and clarified, there mull be nothing but the calf's foot boiled to a hard jelly ; when cold, take off the fat, clear it with the whites of eggs, run it through a flannel bag, and mix it with the clear, which you have faved of the fyllabubs. Sweeten it to your palate, and give it a boil ; then pour it into bafons, or what you pleafe. When cold, turn it out, and it is a fine flummery.

Whipt fyllabub.

RUB a lump of loaf-fugar on the outfide of a lemon, put it into a pint of thin cream, and fweeten it to your tafte. Then put in the juice of a lemon, and a glafs of Madeira wine, or French brandy. Mill it to a froth with a chocolate mill, and take it off as it rifes, and lay it into a hair fieve. Then fill one half of your poffet-glaffes a little more than half full with white wine, and the other half of your glaffes a little more than half full with red wine. Then lay on your froth as high as you can; but take care that it be well drained on your fieve, otherwife it will mix with your wine, and your fyllabub will be thereby fpoiled.

Lemon fyllabub.

RUB a quarter of a pound of loaf-fugar upon the out-rind of two lemons, till you have got all the effence out of them, and then put the fugar into a pint of cream, and the fame quantity of white wine. Squeeze in the juice of both lemons, and let it ftand for two hours. Then mill it with a chocolate mill to raife the froth, and take it off with a fpoon as it rifes, or it, will make it heavy. Lay it upon a hair fieve to drain, then fill your glaffes with the remainder, and lay on the froth as high as you can. Let them ftand all night, and they will be clear at the bottom.

To make a fine Syllabub from the Cow.

Sweeten a quart of cyder with double refined sugar, grate nutmeg into it, then milk your cow into your liquor, when you have thus added what quantity of milk you think proper, pour half a pint or more, in proportion to the quantity of syllabub you make, of the sweetest cream you can get all over it.

The process of whisking or aerating heavy cream causes the cream to become thick and dense creating what is known as Whipped Cream.

There are two ingredients that are used in making both Syllabub and Cheese: Dairy [Milk/Cream] and Acid. When making syllabub, the acid in the recipe [acid in alcohol or lemon juice] is coagulating the milk, cream, or combination of milk and cream, separating the milk solids into curds. The recipe directions are to collect the solids as they separate and rise to the top of the beverage placing them on a sieve to drain. This is the same process as making cheese by allowing the curds to drain in a colander. After removing the "froth" and allowing the beverage to "stand all night" undisturbed, the remaining milk solids will coagulate and rise to the surface leaving the beverage "clear at the bottom".

Recipes also direct the maker to use a "chocolate mill" which is similar to a butter churn. It was a small pitcher with a wooden dasher used to churn or aerate the chocolate drink. Whisking does not have the same result as churning. Whisking or churning cream creates an emulsion which is mixing two ingredients together that don't ordinarily mix. Whipped cream is an air-fat, where butter is a water-fat emulsion. Two separate emulsions resulting in two separate textures and tastes.

Depending on how the syllabub is made, there would have been three different textures and tastes from curd, air-fat emulsion, or water-fat emulsion.

Syllabub

- *For syllabub: Using a mixing bowl, whisk together two tablespoons of granulated sugar, one-half cup of heavy cream, one-quarter cup of liquor [**CIDER** or **WINE**], and one tablespoons of lemon juice. Using a manual whipping cream pump dispenser [milk creamer hand pump], and following the manufacturer's instructions, create a froth. Pour liquor into glasses and top with equal portions of churned cream, or*

- *use a whisk in place of the manual whipping cream pump whisking the cream until thickened, or*

- *stir the ingredients into the beverage allowing the syllabub to stand until the cream has separated. Remove the separated cream or milk solids and place on a fine wire sieve. Allow to drain. Place the cream back on top of the beverage.*

  - Alternate method: Whisk together two tablespoons of granulated sugar, one-half cup of heavy cream, one-quarter cup of **WHITE WINE**, and one tablespoons of lemon juice.

Pies

Apple Pie.

Apple Pie I

Stew and strain the apples, to every three pints, grate the peal of a fresh lemon, add cinnamon, mace, rose-water and sugar to your taste--and bake in paste No. 3.

> Apples, as needed, stewed and strained
> Grated peel of 1 lemon
> Cinnamon, to taste
> Mace, to taste
> Rose water, as needed
> Sugar, to taste
> Paste, as needed

Stewing apples and passing them through a colander removes the peel, core, and seeds creating applesauce. In addition, stewing the apples will reduce the moisture content which is important for a thick sauce to bind the apples together.

> For apple pie I: Peel, quarter, and remove the core from three pounds of Granny Smith apples. Add the apples to a covered stock pot and heat over medium temperature until soft, stirring occasionally to prevent burning. Using a blender, puree the apples. Return the puree to the pot and allow to simmer until thickened to a paste. Whisk in one-quarter cup of **ROSE WATER**, one-third cup of brown sugar, one teaspoon of

ground cinnamon, one-half teaspoon of ground mace, and one tablespoon of grated lemon peel. Prepare **PIE DOUGH** rolling to one-eighth inch thick and line a pie pan. Prebake the pie dough until it starts to brown, about 10 minutes. Spoon the apple filling onto the dough and bake at 350°**F** until the filling is set, about 60 minutes.

Sugar starts to jell at 230°F. In order for the pie to set and not be runny, the internal temperature of the apple pie would need to reach 230°F. Modern recipes use cornstarch to absorb moisture and thicken so the internal temperature is not as crucial and allows for adjustments in sugar content for sweet or tart pies.

A buttered apple Pie.

Apple Pie II

Pare, quarter and core tart apples, lay in paste No. 3, cover with the same; bake half an hour, when drawn, gently raise the top crust, add sugar, butter, cinnamon, mace, wine or rose-water q: s:

>Apples, pared, cored, and quartered
>Paste, as needed
>Sugar, as needed
>Butter, as needed,
>Cinnamon, as needed
>Mace, as needed
>Wine or rose water, as needed

q: s: or q: f: (as much needed-to taste)

❖ Pare and slice apples into quarters removing the core and seeds. Prepare a nine-inch pie pan with **PIE DOUGH** and trim the edge. Place the apples onto the dough. Cover with additional dough pinching the edges with your fingers to seal. Bake at 350°F for 30 minutes. While the pie is baking, create the sugar coating by adding **WINE**, **ROSE WATER**, cinnamon, mace, **BUTTER**, and sugar to a bowl, mixing thoroughly. After the pie has baked 30 minutes, remove it from the oven, and cut away the top and set aside. Drizzle the sugar evenly across the apples and allow to cool.

- The first apple pie was made of unsweetened apples in an inedible shell.

If you remove the top crust and add sugar, it doesn't reach the proper temperature to jell and create a binder for the apples. On the other hand, if you remove the top crust, add sugar and replace the crust, there is too much moisture, and you have thin syrup with the apples.

After baking the pie, the apples are not soft but rather hard and should be at least al dente. It wasn't until a century later when the apples were tossed in a sugar coating prior to placing them on the pie dough, covering, and baking. Using this method allows the sugar to reach proper temperature and jell, softening the apples.

➢ For apple pie II: Pare three pounds of Granny Smith apples and cut each apple into eight slices removing the core and seeds. Combine the apples, one cup of brown sugar, two tablespoons each of cornstarch and melted **BUTTER**, one-quarter cup of **ROSE WATER** or **FORTIFIED WINE**, one tablespoon of grated lemon peel, one teaspoon of ground cinnamon, and one-half teaspoon of ground mace. Using a sauce pot, add the apple mixture and heat over medium temperature, stirring regularly, until the apples are al dente and the syrup has thickened. Remove from heat. Prepare **PIE DOUGH** rolling to one-eighth inch thick and line a pie pan. Prebake the pie dough until it starts to brown, about 10 minutes. Spoon the filling onto the dough and cover with a second portion of dough. Pinch together the edges of the top and bottom portions of the dough. Bake at 350°F until golden brown and the sauce is bubbling, about 60 minutes.

Pompkin.

Pumpkin Pie

No. 1. One quart stewed and strained, 3 pints cream, 9 beaten eggs, sugar, mace, nutmeg and ginger, laid into paste No. 7 or 3, and with a dough spur, cross and chequer it, and baked in dishes three quarters of an hour.

No. 2. One quart of milk, 1 pint pompkin, 4 eggs, molasses, allspice and ginger in a crust, bake 1 hour.

32 ounces pumpkin, stewed and strained
6 cups heavy cream

9 eggs, beaten
Sugar, to taste
Mace, to taste
Nutmeg, to taste
Ginger, to taste
Paste, as needed

- The first recorded recipe for pie consisted of cooked squash.

➢ For pumpkin pie: Whisk together 16 ounces of pumpkin puree, three cups of heavy cream, five beaten eggs, three-quarter cup of brown sugar, one-half teaspoon each of ground mace, ground nutmeg, and ground ginger. Prepare **PIE DOUGH** rolling to one-eighth inch thick and line a pie pan. Pour the pumpkin filling onto the dough and bake at 350°F until the center is set and a toothpick comes clean from the center of the pie.

➢ Alternate method: Whisk together 16 ounces of pumpkin puree, two cups of milk, four beaten eggs, one-half cup of molasses, one-quarter teaspoon of allspice, and one-half teaspoon of ground ginger. Prepare **PIE DOUGH** rolling to one-eighth inch thick and line a pie pan. Pour the pumpkin filling onto the dough and bake at 350°F until the center is set and a toothpick comes clean from the center of the pie.

A Chicken Pie.

Chicken Pot Pie

Pick and clean six chickens, (without scalding) take out their inwards and wash the birds while whole, then joint the birds, salt and pepper the pieces and inwards. Roll one-inch thick paste No. 8 and cover a deep dish, and double at the rim or edge of the dish, put thereto a layer of chickens and a layer of thin slices of butter, till the chickens and one and a half pound butter are expended, which cover with a thick paste; bake one and a half hour. Or if your oven be poor, parboil, the chickens with half a pound of butter, and put the pieces with the remaining one pound of butter, and half the gravy into the paste, and while boiling, thicken the residue of the gravy, and when the pie is drawn, open the crust, and add the gravy.

6 chickens
Salt, as needed
Pepper, as needed
Paste, as needed
Butter, as needed
Gravy, as needed

❖ *For chicken pot pie: Prepare* **BÉCHAMEL** *adding eight ounces of skinless chicken breasts diced small. Prepare* **PIE DOUGH** *and roll to one-eighth inch thick lining 12-ounce buttered ramekins with the dough. Spoon the Béchamel into the ramekins one-quarter inch from the top* *and cover with additional dough pinching the two edges together. Bake at 350°F until dough is golden brown and the sauce is bubbling.*

➤ Alternate method: Use **VELOUTÉ** instead of **BÉCHAMEL**. Add one-quarter cup of medium diced carrots to a sauce pot with enough water to cover. Bring to a boil. Allow to cook until the carrots are al dente. Drain the carrots in a colander and mix them with one-quarter cup of fresh peas. Stir into the Velouté prior to filling the ramekins.

Minced Pie of Beef.
Mincemeat Pie

Four pound boild beef, chopped fine; and salted; six pound of raw apple chopped also, one pound beef suet, one quart of Wine or rich sweet cyder, one ounce mace, and cinnamon, a nutmeg, two pounds raisins, bake in paste No. 3, three fourths of an hour.

4 pounds beef, boiled and minced
6 pounds apples, chopped
16 ounces suet
32 ounces wine or cider
1 ounce mace
1 ounce cinnamon
1 ounce nutmeg
32 ounces raisins
Paste, as needed

- ❖ *For minced pie: Prepare* **PIE DOUGH** *and roll to one-eighth inch thick lining 12-ounce buttered ramekins. Prepare a filling by adding four pounds of bottom round or stew beef, three pounds of Granny Smith apples [peeled, cored, and diced], four cups of* **RED WINE** *or* **CIDER**, *one tablespoon each of ground mace and cinnamon, one teaspoon ground nutmeg, and two cups of raisins to a sauce pot. Add the meat mixture to the ramekins and top with additional dough pinching the two together. Bake at 350°F until dough is golden brown.*

- ➢ Alternate method: Prepare **PIE DOUGH** and roll to one-eighth inch thick, lining 12-ounce buttered ramekins. Prepare a filling by combing in a saucer pan one-quarter cup each of diced carrot and onion, and one pound of bottom round or stew beef, minced and seasoned with salt and ground black pepper. Cook over medium temperature until well browned. Prepare **ESPAGNOLE** while beef is cooking. Combine the Espagnole and beef mixture ladling into the ramekins to one-quarter inch from the top. Cover with additional dough pinching the two pieces of dough together at the edge. Bake at 350°F until dough is golden brown and the sauce is bubbling.

- ➢ Alternate method: Season **ESPAGNOLE** with **WORCESTERSHIRE SAUCE** to taste.

Cakes and Cookies

A trifle.

Trifle

Fill a dish with biscuit finely broken, rusk and spiced cake, wet with wine, then pour a good boil'd custard, (not too thick) over the rusk, and put a syllabub over that; garnish with jelley and flowers.

Savoiardi, as needed
Rusk, as needed
Spiced cake, as needed
Wine, as needed
Custard, as needed
Syllabub, as needed
Jelly as needed
Flowers, as needed

➢ Using a trifle dish, layer starting from the bottom of the dish:

- **SAVOIARDI** broken into pieces,

- stale **WHITE BREAD** broken into pieces,

- drizzle with **FORTIFIED WINE** to soften the savoiardi and stale bread,

- **SPICED CAKE** cut into cubes,

- **PUDDING** spooned over the spice cake,

- **SYLLABUB** spooned over the pudding.

Garnish the dessert with Jelly and edible flowers.

Using a trifle bowl, layer in order savoiardi and white bread. Drizzle enough fortified wine on the breads to soften them. Top the breads with spiced cake, pudding and syllabub.

Milk pancakes.

Crepes

PUT fix or eight eggs, leaving out half the whites, into a quart of milk, and mix them well till your batter be of a fine thickneſs. Obſerve to mix your flour firſt with a little milk, then add the reſt by degrees. Put in two ſpoonfuls of beaten ginger, a glaſs of brandy, and a little ſalt. Stir all together, and make your ſtew-pan very clean. Put in a piece of butter of the ſize of a walnut, and then put in a ladleful of batter, which will make a pancake, moving the pan round, ſo that the batter may be every where even alike in the pan; and when you think that ſide be enough, toſs it, or turn it cleverly without breaking it. When it be done, lay it in a diſh before the fire, and proceed to do the reſt in like manner. Strew a little ſugar over them when you ſend them to table, and take care that they be dry.

6 to 8 eggs
32 ounces milk
Flour, as needed
2 tablespoons ground ginger

8 ounces brandy
Salt, to taste
Butter, as needed
Sugar, as needed

- For crepes: Whisk four egg yolks, two egg whites, one and one-half cups of bread flour, two tablespoons of ground ginger, eight ounces of **BRANDY**, and eight ounces of milk. Season with salt to taste. Heat a sauté pan over medium temperature and brush with **BUTTER**. Ladle batter into the pan and tilt the pan so that batter coats the pan from edge to edge. The crepe should be thin so the amount of batter to ladle will depend on the size of the pan used. When the edge of the batter starts to dry, flip the crepe over to lightly brown the other side. Fold in one-half and in one-half a second time. Sprinkle with powdered sugar.

- Alternate method: Add one tablespoon of sugar with one teaspoon of vanilla extract.

A pound cake.
English Caraway Cake

BEAT a pound of butter in an earthen pan with your hand one way, till it be like a fine thick cream. Then have ready twelve eggs, but leave out half the whites ; beat them well, then beat them up with the butter, a pound of flour beat in it, a pound of fugar, and a few carraways. Beat all well together with your hand for an hour, or you may beat it with a wooden fpoon. Put all into a buttered pan, and bake it in a quick oven for one hour.

16 ounces butter
12 eggs
16 ounces flour
16 ounces sugar
Caraway seed, as needed

- For pound cake: Whisk 16 ounces of **BUTTER** until creamed. Whisk in six eggs, six egg whites, 16 ounces of granulated sugar, 16 ounces of bread flour, and one tablespoon of caraway seeds. Spoon the batter into a buttered cake pan and bake at 350°**F** until a toothpick comes clean when stuck in the middle of the cake and pulled out.

- Alternate method: Omit the caraway seeds and replace with two tablespoons of liquor [brandy, sherry, or rum], and two teaspoons of extract [vanilla or almond]. To lighten the cake, add one and one-half teaspoons of baking powder.

Gingerbread cakes.

Gingerbread Cookie

TAKE three pounds of flour, a pound of fugar, the fame quantity of butter rolled in very fine, two ounces of ginger beat fine, and a large nutmeg grated. Then take a pound of treacle, a quarter of a pint of cream, and make them warm together. Make up the bread ftiff, roll it put, and make it up into thin cakes. Cut them out with a tea-cup or fmall glafs, or roll them round like nuts, and bake them in a slack oven on tin plates.

48 ounces flour
16 ounces sugar
16 ounces butter
2 ounces ground ginger
1 teaspoon ground nutmeg
16 ounces molasses
4 ounces heavy cream

- ❖ *For gingerbread cookies: Whisk eight ounces of **BUTTER** with eight ounces of brown sugar. Combine the butter with 24 ounces of bread flour, one and one-half teaspoons of ground ginger, and one teaspoon of ground nutmeg. Using a mixing bowl, combine 16 ounces of molasses with eight ounces of heavy cream. Combine the molasses and flour mixtures. Divide the dough into one and one-half ounce portions. Roll each portion of dough into a round ball and place onto a baking sheet pan lined with parchment paper. Bake at 350°F until firm to touch about 30 minutes.*

- ➢ Alternate method: Replace the flour with pastry flour and add two teaspoons of cinnamon and one teaspoon of ground cloves.

Lemon Cakes.

Lemon Chiffon Cake

TAKE the whites of ten eggs, put to them three fpoonfuls of rofe or orange flower water, and beat them an hour with a whifk. Then put in a pound of beaten and fifted fugar, and grate into it the rind of a lemon. When it be well mixed, put in the juice of half a lemon, and the yolks of ten eggs beat fmooth. Juft before you put it into the oven, ftir in three quarters of a pound of flour, butter your pan, put put it into a moderate oven, and an hour will bake it. You may, if you choofe it, make orange cake in the fame manner.

>10 eggs
>3 tablespoons rose or orange water
>16 ounces powdered sugar
>Grated peel of 1 lemon
>Juice of half lemon
>12 ounces flour
>Butter, as needed

- ❖ *For lemon cake: Whisk 10 egg whites with three tablespoons of* **ROSE WATER** *to stiff peaks. Slowly whisk in 16 ounces of powdered sugar, two tablespoons of lemon juice, and the peel of a grated lemon. Using a separate bowl, whisk together 12 ounces of bread flour with 10 egg yolks until smooth. Fold the flour mixture into the egg whites and spoon into a buttered cake pan. Bake at 350°F until a toothpick comes clean when stuck in the middle of* *the cake and pulled out.*

- ❖ *Alternate method: Sift together 12 ounces of cake flour and one tablespoon of baking powder and set aside. Whisk 10 egg whites with three tablespoons of* **ROSE WATER** *to stiff peaks. Slowly whisk in 16 ounces of powdered sugar, and the peel of a grated lemon. Using a separate bowl, whisk together 10 egg yolks, six ounces of water, and 2 ounces of lemon juice. Whisk the egg yolks with the flour mixture until smooth. Fold the flour and egg whites together and spoon into a buttered cake pan. Bake at 350°F until a toothpick comes clean when stuck in the middle of the cake and pulled out.*

- ❖ *Alternate method: Use orange juice and grated orange peel instead of lemon juice and grated lemon peel.*

This cake resembles an Angel Food Cake; however, egg yolks are added when baking a Chiffon Cake.

Cheefecakes.

New York Cheesecake

PUT a fpoonful of runnet into a quart of new milk, and fet it near the fire. Let the milk be blood warm, and when it be broken, drain the curd through a coarfe fieve. Now and then break the curd gently with your fingers, and rub into it a quarter of a pound of butter, the fame quantity of fugar, a nutmeg, and two Naples bifcuits grated; the yolks of four eggs and the white of one, and an ounce of almonds well beaten with two fpoonfuls of rofe water, and

the fame of fack. Clean fix ounces of currants well, and put them into your curd. Mix all well together, and fend it to the oven.

Rennet
Milk
16 ounces butter
16 ounces sugar
1 teaspoon nutmeg
2 Naples biscuits
4 eggs
1-ounce almonds, ground
2 tablespoons rose water
2 tablespoons wine
6 ounces currants

- Recipes for lemon and orange cheesecakes can be found in 18TH century cooking. Adding a spoonful of runnet [rennet] to new milk will separate the milk fat leaving just soft curds similar to cream cheese.

- *For cheesecake: Whisk together eight ounces of **CREAM CHEESE**, two eggs, one-quarter cup each of granulated sugar and grated **SAVOIARDI**, two tablespoons each of **ROSE WATER**, port wine, and ground almonds. Prepare* PIE DOUGH *rolling to one-eighth inch thick and line a pie pan. Pour the batter onto the pie dough and bake at 275°F until center of cake is set and toothpick comes clean when stuck in the middle of the cake and pulled out.*

- Alternate method: Whisk together eight ounces of **CREAM CHEESE**, two eggs, one-quarter cup each of granulated sugar and bread flour, and one-half cup of lemon or orange juice concentrate. Prepare **PIE DOUGH** rolling to one-eighth inch thick and line a pie pan. Pour the batter onto the pie dough and bake at 275°F until the center of cake is set and toothpick comes out clean when stuck in the middle of the cake.

Note: You can use other juice concentrates (limeade, Bacardi® Mixers Strawberry or Peach Daiquiri) for flavoring in the cheesecake.

A rich Cake.

Raisin Butter Cake

Rub 2 pound of butter into 5 pound of flour, add 15 eggs (not much beaten) 1 pint of emptins, 1 pint of wine, kneed up stiff like biscuit, cover well and put by and let rise over night. To 2 and a half pound raisins, add 1 gill brandy, to soak over night, or if new half an hour in the morning, add them with 1 gill rose-water and 2 and half pound of loaf sugar, 1 ounce cinnamon, work well and bake as loaf cake, No. 1.

32 ounces of butter
80 ounces of flour
15 eggs
16 ounces emptins
16 ounces wine
40 ounces raisins
5 ounces brandy

4 ounces rose water
40 ounces sugar
1 ounce cinnamon

❖ *For raisin butter cake: Soak one-half cup of raisins in **BRANDY** until soft. Whisk together 12 ounces each of **BUTTER** and granulated sugar, four large eggs, and one-half teaspoon of salt. In a separate bowl, whisk together 15 ounces of bread flour, four and one-half teaspoons of active dry yeast, 13 ounces of **WHITE WINE**, one-quarter cup each of **ROSE WATER** and raisins, and one teaspoon of cinnamon. Whisk the butter and flour mixtures together. Butter a loaf pan and spoon in the batter. Bake at 350°F until the center of bread is set and toothpick comes out clean when stuck in the middle of the cake and pulled out.*

➢ Alternate method: Use cake flour instead of bread flour and replace the active dry yeast with baking powder.

The butter should always be at room temperature before mixing [creaming] together with sugar.

Johny Cake, or Hoe Cake.
Cornbread

Scald 1 pint of milk and put to 3 pints of Indian meal, and half pint of flower--bake before the fire. Or scald with milk two thirds of the Indian meal, or wet two thirds with boiling water, add

salt, molasses and shortening, work up with cold water pretty stiff, and bake as above.

16 ounces milk
48 ounces cornmeal
8 ounces flour

- ❖ *For cornbread: Whisk together five large eggs, two cups of milk, two tablespoons of corn syrup, one-quarter cup of granulated sugar, and three-fourth cup of melted **BUTTER**. In a separate bowl, combine ten ounces each of bread flour and cornmeal, two tablespoons of baking powder, and one teaspoon of salt. Whisk the egg and flour mixtures together. Butter a square baking pan and spoon in the batter. Bake at 350°F until the center of bread is set and toothpick comes clean when stuck in the middle of the bread and pulled out.*

- ❖ *Alternate method: Replace granulated sugar with molasses.*

- ➢ Alternate method: Mix in one-quarter cup diced jalapeno peppers.

Corn Pudding

- ❖ Alternate method: Strain one 15 ounce can of creamed corn discarding the kernels and adding the cream, one-quarter cup of granulated sugar, and one egg to the **CORNBREAD** mixture. Bake at 350°F until center is set.

Queens Cake.

Queens Cake aka modern Gingerbread Cake

Whip half pound butter to a cream, add 1 pound sugar, ten eggs, one glass wine, half gill rose-water, and spices to your taste, all worked into one and a quarter pound flour, put into pans, cover with paper, and bake in a quick well heat oven, 12 or 16 minutes.

> 8 ounces butter
> 16 ounces sugar
> 10 eggs
> 8 ounces white wine
> 2-1/2 ounces rose water
> Spices, to taste

- ❖ *For Queens Cake: Prepare* **GINGERBREAD** *whisking in eight ounces of white wine and two tablespoons of baking powder. Butter a cake pan and spoon in the batter. Bake at 350°F until the center of bread is set and toothpick comes clean when stuck in the middle of the bread and pulled out.*
- ➢ Alternate method: Use cake flour instead of bread flour. Reduce the brown sugar to 18 ounces and add 18 ounces of molasses.

Icings for Cakes.

Cake Icing

TAKE a pound of double-refined fugar pounded and fifted fine, and mix it with the whites of twenty four eggs, in an earthen pan. Whifk them well for two or three hours till it looks white and thick, and then, with a thin broad board, or bunch of feathers, fpread it all over the top and fides of the cake. Set it at a proper diftance before a clear fire, and keep turning it continually that it may not turn colour ; but a cool oven is beft, where an hour will harden it. Or you may make your icing thus : Beat the whites of three eggs to a ftrong froth, beat a pound of Jordan almonds very fine with 'rofe water, and mix your almonds with the eggs lightly together. Then beat a pound of loaf fugar very fine, and put it in by degrees. When your cake be enough, take it out, lay on your icing, and proceed as above directed.

16 ounces powdered sugar
24 eggs

- ❖ *For cake icing: Whisk 24 egg whites to stiff peaks and slowly whisk in 16 ounces of powdered sugar.*
- ➢ Alternate method: Whisk three egg whites until they start to stiffen. Grind 16 ounces of almonds to a powder and combine with enough **ROSE WATER** to make a paste. Whisk the almond

165

powder into the egg whites. Briskly whisk the egg whites to stiff peaks while slowly adding 16 ounces of powdered sugar.

Macaroons.

Macaroons

TAKE a pound of fweet almonds blanched and beaten, and put to them a pound of fugar, and a little rofe water to keep them from oiling. Then beat the whites of feven eggs to a froth, and put them in, and beat them well together. Drop them on wafer paper, grate fugar over them, and put them into the oven.

> 16 ounces almonds
> 16 ounces sugar
> Rose water, as needed
> 7 eggs, separated

Meringues are flourless. Macarons contain almond flour, and like meringues, they are piped onto a baking sheet pan. Macaroons contain almond flour; however, they are dropped or spooned onto a baking sheet pan instead of uniformly piped. To create almond flour, beat or grind almonds to a powder.

> ➢ For macaroons: Whisk seven egg whites to a froth and set aside. Grind 16 ounces of almonds to a powder and combine with 16 ounces of

granulated sugar and enough **ROSE WATER** to make a paste. Fold the paste into the egg whites. Whisk the egg whites to stiff peaks. Using a spoon, drop portions of the egg whites onto a baking sheet pan coated with non-stick cooking spray. Sprinkle with granulated sugar and bake at 250°F until dry and light in weight.

Cookies.

Sugar Cookie

One pound sugar boiled slowly in half pint water, scum well and cool, add two tea spoons pearl ash dissolved in milk, then two and half pounds flour, rub in 4 ounces butter, and two large spoons of finely powdered coriander seed, wet with above; make roles half an inch thick and cut to the shape you please; bake fifteen or twenty minutes in a slack oven--good three weeks.

16 ounces sugar
8 ounces of water
2 teaspoons pearl ash
40 ounces of bread flour
4 ounces of butter
2 tablespoons ground coriander seed

> For sugar cookies: Whisk together 10 ounces each of **BUTTER** and granulated sugar and one teaspoon of salt. In a separate bowl, whisk together one large egg, one-quarter cup of

milk, and three-quarter teaspoon of ground coriander seed. Whisk the milk and butter mixtures with 12 ounces of bread flour and one tablespoon of baking powder. Flour a board and roll the dough to three-eighth inch thick. Cut into desired shape and bake at 375°F until light golden brown.

Gingerbread.

Gingerbread

No. 4. Three pound sugar, half pound butter, quarter of a pound of ginger, one doz. eggs, one glass rose water, rub into three pounds flour, bake as No. 1.

48 ounces sugar
8 ounces butter
4 ounces ginger
12 eggs
8 ounces rose water
48 ounces flour

❖ *For gingerbread: Whisk together until smooth, 36 ounces of bread flour, two tablespoons of ground ginger, one-quarter cup of soft butter, three eggs, one-quarter cup of rose water, and 36 ounces of brown sugar. Refrigerate for 24 hours. On a well-floured board, roll the dough to a one-quarter inch thick square. Cut into desired shapes and place onto a baking sheet pan lined with parchment paper. Bake at 350°F until crisp.*

Tarts and Puffs

Wafers

Pizzelles

TAKE a fpoonful of orange flower water, two fpoonfuls of flour, two of fugar, and the fame of cream. Beat them well together for half an hour; then make your wafer tongs hot, and pour a little of your batter in to cover your irons. Bake them on a ftove fire, and as they be baking, roll them round a ftick like a fpiggot. When they be cold, they will be very crifp, and are very proper to be eat with jellies, or with tea.

> 1 tablespoon orange water
> 2 tablespoons flour
> 2 tablespoons sugar
> 2 tablespoons heavy cream

- For pizzelles: Whisk together two tablespoons each of bread flour, granulated sugar, and heavy cream, and one tablespoon of **ORANGE WATER**. Follow the manufacturer's directions for a pizzelle press.

- Alternate method: Whisk together three-quarter cup of granulated sugar, eight tablespoons of melted butter, one tablespoon of orange extract, and three eggs. Whisk granulated sugar mixture with one and one-half cups of bread flour until smooth.

Sugar puff's.
Meringue Cookie

BEAT the whites of ten eggs till they rife to a high froth. Then put them in a marble mortar or wooden bowl, and add as much double-refined fugar as will make it thick ; then rub it round the mortar for half an hour, put in a few carraway feeds, and take a fheet of wafers, and lay it on as broad as a fix-pence, and as high as you can. Put them into a moderately-heated oven half a quarter of an hour, and they will look as white as fnow.

10 eggs, whites
Powdered sugar, as needed
Caraway seed, as needed

➢ For meringue: Whisk together 10 egg whites to stiff peaks. Slowly whisk in two and one-half cups of powdered sugar with two teaspoons of ground caraway seed to stiff peaks. Line a baking sheet pan with parchment paper. Spoon the meringue onto the pan three-quarter inch wide with three-quarter inch spacing. Bake at 325°F until firm to touch. Remove and allow to cool.

Lemon Puffs.

Lemon Meringue Cookie

TAKE a pound of double-refined fugar, beat it, and fift it through a fine fieve. Put it into a bowl, with the juice of two lemons, and beat them together. Then beat the white of an egg to a very high froth. Put it into your bowl, beat it half an hour, and then put in three eggs, with two rinds of lemons grated. Mix it well up, throw fugar on your papers, drop on the puffs in fmall drops, and bake them in an oven moderately hot.

> 16 ounces powdered sugar
> Juice of two lemons
> 1 egg, white
> 3 eggs
> Grated peel of 2 lemons

> Prepare **MERINGUE COOKIE** using two teaspoons of lemon extract instead of the caraway seed.

> Alternate method: Use vanilla, mint, or orange extract instead of lemon extract.

Apple Tarts.

Apple Tart

Stew and strain the apples, add cinnamon, rose-water, wine and sugar to your taste, lay in paste, royal, squeeze thereon orange juice---bake gently.

Apples, stewed
Cinnamon, to taste
Rose water, as needed
Wine, as needed
Sugar, as needed
Paste, royal, as needed
Orange juice, as needed

> For apple tart: Prepare **FRIED APPLES** and set aside. Prepare **PUFF PASTRY** rolling to one-eighth inch thick and docking the dough by using a fork and poking little holes all over the dough. Line a tart pan with the dough. Prebake the pie dough until it starts to brown, about 10 minutes. Spoon the fried apples onto the dough, drizzle with orange juice, and bake at 350°**F** until the dough is light brown and the apples are bubbling.

Orange or Lemon Tart.

Lemon or Orange Tart

Take 6 large lemons, rub them well in salt, put them into salt and water and let rest 2 days,

change them daily in fresh water, 14 days, then cut slices and mince as fine as you can and boil them 2 or 3 hours till tender, then take 6 pippins, pare, quarter and core them, boil in 1 pint fair water till the pippins break, then put the half of the pippins, with all the liquor to the orange or lemon, and add one pound sugar, boil all together one quarter of an hour, put into a gallipot and squeeze thereto a fresh orange, one spoon of which, with a spoon of the pulp of the pippin, laid into a thin royal paste, laid into small shallow pans or saucers, brushed with melted butter, and some superfine sugar sifted thereon, with a gentle baking, will be very good.

6 large lemons or oranges
Salt, as needed
Water, as needed
6 Pippins (apples)
16 ounces sugar
1 tablespoon fresh orange juice
Royal Paste, as needed

Putting the lemons or oranges in salt brine for 14 days will draw out the moisture in the fruit concentrating the flavor and removing the bitter taste of the peel. Boiling apples in water can substitute for apple cider. To create a flavored syrup, add sugar to the juice of lemons or oranges along with the apple cider and bring to a boil. Pour onto pastry dough and bake. When the flavored syrup reaches 248°F, the syrup jells to jam or jelly. This recipe could easily be created by spooning lemon or orange jam over pie dough and baking until the dough is light brown.

- For lemon or orange tart: Whisk together one-quarter cup of granulated sugar, one-half cup of lemon juice, the grated peel of one lemon, four large eggs, and one-quarter cup of heavy cream. Prepare **PUFF PASTRY** rolling to one-eighth inch thick, docking the dough by using a fork and poking little holes all over the dough. Line a tart pan with the dough. Prebake the pie dough until it starts to turn off-white in color, about 10 minutes. Pour the filling onto the dough and bake at 300°**F** until the dough is light brown and the filling is set.

- Alternate method: Substitute orange juice and peel for the lemon juice and peel.

- Alternate method: Top with syllabub.

Custards and Creams

Plain Cuftards.

English Pudding

SET a quart of good cream over a flow fire, with a little cinnamon, and four ounces of fugar. When it has boiled, take it off the fire, beat the yolks of eight eggs, and put to them a fpoonful of orange flower water, to prevent the cream from cracking. Stir them in by degrees as your cream cools, put the pan over a very flow fire, ftir it carefully one way till it be almoft boiling, and then pour it into cups.

Or you may make your cuftards in this manner: Take a quart of new milk, fweeten it to your tafte, beat up well the yolks of eight eggs and the whites of four. Stir them into the milk, and bake it in China bafons. Or put them in a deep China difh, and pour boiling water round them, till the water be better than half way up their fides; but take care the water does not boil too faft, left it fhould get into your cups, and fpoil your cuftards.

32 ounces heavy cream
Cinnamon, as needed
4 ounces of sugar
8 egg yolks
1 tablespoon orange water

> For pudding: Whisk eight egg yolks with one-quarter cup of granulated sugar, one teaspoon of cinnamon, one-quarter cup of corn starch, and one tablespoon of **ORANGE WATER**. In the upper pot of a double boiler, add 32 ounces of cream. Bring to a boil. Briskly whisk the eggs while slowly pouring in the hot cream. Return the cream to the upper pot. Bring water in the lower pot to a boil. Reduce the temperature to medium. Place the upper pot onto the lower pot. Continue whisking the cream until thickened. Portion the cream into dishes and allow to cool.

Orange Cuftards.

English Orange Pudding

HAVING boiled very tender the rind of half a Seville orange, beat it in a mortar till it be very fine. Put to it a fpoonful of the beft brandy, the juice of a Seville orange, four ounces of loaf fugar, and the yolks of four eggs. Beat them all well together for ten minutes, and then pour in by degrees a pint of boiling cream. Keep beating them till they be cold, then put them in cuftard cups, and fet them in an earthen difh of hot water. Let them ftand till they fet, then take them out, and ftick preferved orange on the top. They may be ferved up either hot or cold.

> Follow the recipe for **ENGLISH PUDDING** omitting the cinnamon and **ORANGE WATER** replacing them with one tablespoon of **BRANDY** and two tablespoons of orange extract.

Lemon Cuftards.

Crème Brûlée

TAKE half a pound of double-refined fugar, the juice of two lemons, the out-rind of one pared very thin, the inner-rind of one boiled tender and rubbed through a fieve, and a pint of white wine. Let them boil a good while, then take out the peel and a little of the liquor, and fet it to cool. Pour the reft into the difh you intend for it, beat four yolks and two whites of eggs, and mix them with your cool liquor. Strain them into your difh, ftir them well up together, and let them on a flow fire in boiling water. When it be enough, grate the rind of a lemon all over the top, and you may brown it over with a hot falamander. This, like the former, may be eaten either hot or cold.

> 8 ounces powdered sugar
> Juice of 2 lemons
> 2 grated lemon peels
> 1 grated lemon pith
> 1 cup white wine
> 4 eggs, separated

> For Crème Brûlée: Whisk eight egg yolks with one-quarter cup of granulated sugar, one tablespoon of **BRANDY**, and one teaspoon of lemon extract. Place 32 ounces of heavy cream in a sauce pot and bring to a boil. Briskly whisk eggs while slowly pouring in the hot cream. Portion the cream into ramekins and put

them into a roasting pan. Pour enough water in the pan to cover halfway up the side of the ramekins. Heat the water over medium-high temperature until it starts to steam and then place the lid on the roasting pan. Reduce the temperature to medium-low. Do not allow the water to boil. Allow to steam for 30 minutes. Remove the ramekins and allow to cool to room temperature. Sprinkle the custard with granulated sugar. Using a mini butane torch, slowly heat the sugar until it caramelizes or has turned medium brown in color.

CUSTARDS.

Custard

2. Sweeten a quart of milk, add nutmeg, wine, brandy, rose-water and six eggs; bake in tea cups or dishes, or boil in water, taking care that it don't boil into the cups.

6 eggs, beaten
32 ounces milk
4 ounces brown sugar
1 ounce dessert wine
1 ounce brandy
1 ounce rose water
1/2 teaspoon ground nutmeg

➤ For custard: Whisk six eggs with one-quarter cup of brown sugar, two tablespoons each of port wine, **BRANDY, ROSE WATER,** and one-half teaspoon of ground nutmeg. Using a sauce pot, add four cups of milk bringing to a boil. Briskly whisk the eggs while slowly pouring in the hot milk. Portion the cream into ramekins and put them into a roasting pan. Pour enough water into the pan covering halfway up the side of the ramekins. Heat the water over medium temperature until the water starts to steam and then place the lid on the roasting pan. Reduce the temperature to medium-low. Do not allow the water to boil. Allow to steam for 30 minutes. Remove the ramekins and allow to cool.

Whipt cream.

Whipped Cream

TAKE the whites of eight eggs, a quart of thick cream, and half a pint of fack. Mix it together, and fweeten it to your tafte with double-refined fugar. You may perfume it, if you pleafe, with a little mufk or ambergris tied in a rag, and fteeped a little in the cream. Whip it up with a whifk, and fome lemon peel tied in the middle of the whifk. Take the froth with a fpoon, and lay it in your glaffes or bafons. This makes a pretty appearance over fine tarts.

8 egg whites
32 ounces of heavy cream
8 ounces of wine
Powdered sugar, as needed
Lemon peel, as needed
Perfume, as needed

- For whipped cream, combine eight ounces of heavy cream, one-quarter cup each of **WHITE WINE**, egg whites, granulated sugar, and three-quarter teaspoon of lemon juice. Whip the cream to stiff peaks. For the perfume, add one-half teaspoon of extract [vanilla, orange, coconut, peppermint, banana] or to your taste.

- Alternate method: Whip the egg whites to stiff peaks. Add remaining ingredients whipping again to stiff peaks.

To make various flavors of ice-cream

Ice cream.

Apricot Ice-Cream

TAKE twelve ripe apricots, pare, done, and fcald them, and beat them fine in a marble mortar. Put to them fix ounces of double-refined fugar, a pint of fcalding cream, and work it through a hair fieve. Put it into a tin that has a clofe cover, and fet it in a tub of ice broken fmall, and a large quantity of falt put among it. When you fee your cream grows thick round the edges of your tin, ftir it, and fet it in again till it grows quite thick. When your cream be all frozen up, take it out of the tin, and put it into the mould you intend it to be turned out of. Then put on the lid, and have ready another tub, with falt and ice in it as before. Put your mould in the middle, and lay your ice under and over it. Let it ftand four or five hours, and dip your tin in warm water when you turn it out; but if it be fummer, remember not to turn it out till the moment you want it. If you have not apricots, any other fruit will anfwer the purpofe, provided you take care to work them very fine in your mortar.

Lemon cream.

Lemon Ice-Cream

TAKE the rinds of two lemons pared very thin, the juice of three, and a pint of fpring-water. Beat the whites of fix eggs very fine, and mix them with the water and lemon. Then fugar it to your tafte, and keep ftirring it till it thickens, but take care that you do not fuffer it to boil. Strain it through a cloth, beat the yolks of fix eggs, and put it over the fire to thicken. 'Ehen pour it into a bowl, and put it into your glaffes as foon as it be cold.

Orange cream.

Orange Ice-Cream

PARE off the rind of a Seville orange very fine, and fqueeze the juice of four oranges. Put them into a toffing-pan, with a pint of water, and eight ounces of fugar. Beat the white of five eggs, and mix all, and let them over the fire. Stir it one way till it grows thick and white, then drain it through a gauze, and ftir it till it be cold. Then beat the yolks of five eggs exceedingly fine, and put it into your pan, with fome cream. Stir it over a very flow fire till it be ready to boil, then put it into a bafon to cool, and having flirred it till it be quite cold, put it into your glaffes.

Chocolate cream.

Chocolate Ice-Cream

TAKE a quarter of a pound of the beft chocolate, and having fcraped it fine, put to it as much water as will diffolve it. Then beat it half an hour in a mortar, and put in as much fine fugar as will fweeten it, and a pint and a half of cream. Mill it, and as the froth rifes, lay it on a fieve. Put the remainder of your cream in poffet glaffes, and lay the frothed cream upon them.

> Ripe fruit, pureed or chocolate
> Powdered sugar
> Heavy cream
> Water
> Eggs

The ingredients for making ice-cream have not changed for over 200 years.

> - For ice-cream base: Whisk 12 egg yolks with one and one-half cups of granulated sugar. Whisk in four cups of whole milk. Using a double boiler, heat the milk, stirring regularly, until the milk has slightly thickened or temperature

reaches 180°F. Remove and allow to cool to room temperature. Whisk in two cups of heavy cream, and a pinch of salt.

- For vanilla: add two teaspoons of vanilla extract.

- For apricot: Peel and remove the skin from ripe apricots. Using a blender, puree the fruit. Reduce the egg yolks to six and add one and one-half cups of apricot puree with three-quarter cup of granulated sugar to the ice cream base. Omit the vanilla extract and replace with lemon juice.

- For lemon or orange: Reduce the heavy cream to three-quarter cup. Add one-quarter cup of lemon or orange juice concentrate, and one cup of granulated sugar to the base omitting the vanilla extract.

- For chocolate: Reduce the granulated sugar to one cup plus two tablespoons and the heavy cream to one and one-half cups. Melt four ounces each of bittersweet and unsweetened chocolate in a double boiler and slowly whisk it into the ice-cream base.

Follow the directions provided by the manufacturer of your ice-cream machine. Spoon ice-cream into a freezer safe container and allow to freeze for 24 hours.

Fritters

Common fritters.

Basic Fritter

GET the largeft baking apples you can, pare them, and take out the core with an apple-fcraper. Cut them in round dices, and dip them in batter made thus. Take half a pint of ale and two eggs, and beat in as much flour as will make it rather thicker than a common pudding, with nutmeg and fugar to your tafte. Let it ftand three or four minutes to rife. Having dipped your apple into this batter, fry them crifp, and ferve them up with fugar grated over them, and wine fauce in a boat.

Apple Fritters.

Apple Fritter

HAVING beat the yolks of eight eggs and the whites of four well together, ftrain them into a pan. Then take a quart of cream, and make it as hot as you can bear your finger in. Then put to it a quarter of a pint of fack, three quarters of a pint of ale, and make a poff'et of it. When it be cool, put to it your eggs, beating it well together. Then put in falt, ginger, nutmeg, and flour, to your liking. Having made

your batter pretty thick, put in pippins diced or pared, and fry them quick in a good deal of batter.

8 eggs, separated
32 ounces heavy cream
4 ounces wine
12 ounces ale
Salt, as needed
Ginger, as needed
Nutmeg, as needed
Flour, as needed
Apples, diced

At some point in time, we have all heard the term Beer Batter. This recipe is the perfect example of a batter made with beer.

Fritter Batter

- For fritter batter: Using a bowl, combine one cup plus two tablespoons of bread flour, one tablespoon of granulated sugar, one-quarter teaspoon each of ground nutmeg, ground ginger, and baking powder. In a separate bowl, whisk one cup of ale, two eggs, and one-quarter teaspoon of vanilla extract. Combine the flour and the ale mixtures briskly whisking together to a thick batter.
- For apple fritters I, prepare **FRITTER BATTER**. Pare, core, and slice apples one-quarter inch thick. Using a stock pot, add enough fry oil to a

one-inch depth and heat to 350°F. Dip each slice of apple into the batter and fry until golden brown on both sides. For the sauce, using a stock pot, combine two cups of powdered sugar with three tablespoons of **RED** or **WHITE WINE**. Heat over medium temperature, while whisking, until the sugar has dissolved and then bring to a hard boil. Spoon the syrup over the fritters and allow to cool.

> For apple fritters II, prepare **FRITTER BATTER** and set aside. Pare, core, and large dice one apple combining with the batter. Using a stock pot, add enough fry oil to one-inch depth and heat to 350°F. Spoon the batter into the oil and fry until golden brown on both sides. For the glaze, using a sauce pot, combine two cups of powdered sugar with three tablespoons of water. Heat over medium temperature, while whisking, until the sugar has dissolved and then bring to a hard boil. Spoon the syrup over the fritters and allow to cool.

To make Curd Fritters.

Cheese Fritter

BOIL a handful of curds, a handful of flour, ten eggs well beaten and ftrained, fome fugar, fome cloves, mace, nut-meg and a little faffron ; ftir all well together, and fry them in very hot beef dripping ; drop them in the pan by fpoonfuls ; ftir them about till they are of a fine yellow brown ; drain them from the fuet, and fcrape fugar on them, when you ferve them up.

➤ For curd fritters: Prepare **FRITTER BATTER** and set aside. Prepare **CHEDDAR CHEESE**; however, after making the cheese curds, do not press the curds into a mold. Combine one-half cup of curds with the fritter batter. Use a stock pot and add enough fry oil to a one-inch depth and heat to 350°F. Spoon the batter into the oil and fry until golden brown on both sides. For the glaze, using a sauce pot, combine two cups of powdered sugar with one-quarter cup of heavy cream. Heat over medium temperature, while whisking, until the sugar has dissolved and then bring to a hard boil. Spoon the syrup over the fritters and allow to cool.

Pickling and Preserves

Common vinegar.

White Vinegar

PUT as many pounds of coarfe Lifbon fugar as you take gallons of water; boil it, and keep fkimming it as long as any fcum will rife. Then put it into tubs, and when it be as cold as beer to work, to it a large piece of bread, and rub it over with yest. Let it work twenty four hours; then have ready a veffel, iron-hooped and well painted, fixed in a place where the fun has full power, and fix it fo as not to have any occafion to move it. When you draw it off, fill your veffels, and lay a tile on the bunghole to keep the dull out. Make it in March, and it will be fit to ufe in June or July. Then draw it off into little ftone bottles, let it hand till you want to ufe it, and it will never be foul any more; but fhould you find it not four enough, let it ftand a month longer before you draw it off.

> For vinegar: Using a stock pot, combine one gallon of water with one and one-half cups of granulated sugar. Bring to a boil. Remove from heat and allow to cool to room temperature. Add one package [5g, .176oz, or one and one-quarter teaspoon] of brewer's yeast. Cover pot with cheese cloth and allow to rest in a cool area. After three months, your vinegar should be ready for canning. Strain through a coffee filter and bottle. Follow the canning directions provided by your canning supplier.

Red cabbage.

Sauerkraut

HAVING fliced your cabbage crofs-ways, put it on an earthen difh, and fprinkle a handful of falt over it. Cover it with another difh, and let it ftand twenty-four hours. Then put it into a cullender to drain, and lay it in your jar. Take white wine vinegar enough to cover it, a little cloves, mace, and a'lfpice. Put them in whole, with a little cochineal bruifed fine. Then boil it up, and pour it either hot or cold on your cabbage. Cover it clofe with a cloth till it be cold, if you pour on the pickle hot, and then tie it up clofe as you do other pickles.

> For sauerkraut: Finely shred cabbage into thin strands and place in a bowl. For every pound of cabbage, add one and one-half teaspoons of non-iodized salt, mixing thoroughly. Allow cabbage to rest 24 hours. For the canning brine, using a stock pot, combine 24 ounces of distilled water, nine ounces of 5% white **VINEGAR**, one and one-half teaspoons ground allspice, one-quarter teaspoon ground clove, and one-half teaspoon of ground mace. Bring to a boil. Your cabbage is ready to be canned using the canning brine. Follow the canning directions provided by your canning supplier.

Cucumbers.

Sweet Pickles

TAKE the greeneft cucumbers, and the moft free from feeds you can get ; fome fmall, to preferve whole, and others large to cut into pieces. Put them into ftrong falt and water in a ftraight mouthed jar, with a cabbage-leaf to keep them down. Set them in a warm place till they be yellow, then wafh them out, and fet them over the fire in frefh water, with a little falt, and a frefh cabbage-leaf over them. Cover the pan very clofe, but take care they do not boil. If they be not of a fine green, change your water, and that will help them. Then cover them as before, and make them hot. When they become of a good green, take them off the fire, and let them ftand till they be cold. Then cut the large ones in quarters, take out the feeds and foft part, then put them into cold water, and let them ftand two days; but change the water twice every day to take out the falt. Take a pound of fingle-refined fugar, and half a pint of water. Set it over the fire, and when you have fkimmed it clean, put in the rind of a lemon, and an ounce of ginger, with the outfide fcraped off, when your fyrup be pretty thick, take it off; and when it be cold, wipe the cucumbers dry, and put them in. Boil the fyrup once in two or three days for three weeks, and ftrengthen the fyrup, if re-quired ; for the grateft danger of fpoiling them is at firft. When you put the fyrup to your cucumbers, be fure that it be quite cold.

➢ For sweet pickles: For the salt brine, combine 64 ounces of distilled water with 16 ounces non-iodized salt. Bring to a boil. Allow to cool to room temperature. Place the cucumbers into the brine and weight them down below the water line for 24 hours. After 24 hours, remove the pickles from brine and wash them with cold water to remove excess salt. For the canning brine, using a sauce pot, combine two cups of 5% white **VINEGAR**, one cup of granulated sugar, peel of one lemon grated, two tablespoons of ground ginger, and one teaspoon each of mustard seed and black peppercorns. Bring to a boil. Allow to cool to room temperature and strain through a coffee filter. Your pickles are ready to be canned using the canning brine. Follow the canning directions provided by your canning supplier.

Gerkins.

Pickled Cucumbers

TAKE a large earthen pan with fpring water in it, and to every gallon of water put two pounds of falt. Mix them well together, and throw in live hundred gerkins. In two hours take them out, and put them to drain. Let them be drained very dry, and then put them into a jar. Put into a pot a gallon of the beft white-wine vinegar, half an ounce of cloves and mace, an ounce of allfpice, the fame quantity of muftard feed, a ftick of horfe-radifh cut in dices, fix bay leaves, two or three races of ginger, a nutmeg cut in pieces, and a handful of falt. Boil up all together

in the pot, and pour it over the gerkins. Cover them clofe down, and let them ftand, twenty-four hours. Then put them in your pot, and let them fimmer over the fire till they be green; but be careful not to let them boil, as that will fpoil them. Then put them into your jar, and cover them clofe down till they be cold. Then tie them over with a bladder and a leather, and put them in a cold dry place.

> For gherkins: For the salt brine, using a stock pot, combine 64 ounces of distilled water with 16 ounces of non-iodized salt. Bring to a boil. Allow to cool to room temperature. Place the cucumbers in the brine and weight down below the water line for 24 hours. After 24 hours, remove the pickles from the brine washing them with cold water to remove excess salt. For the canning brine, using a sauce pot, combine 64 ounces of 5% white **VINEGAR**, one and one-half teaspoons each of ground cloves and mace, one tablespoon each of allspice and mustard seed, three bay leaves, eight ounces of grated horseradish, one whole nutmeg crushed, and two tablespoons of ground ginger. Bring to a boil. Allow to cool to room temperature. Strain through a coffee filter. Your pickles are ready to be canned using the canning brine. Follow the canning directions provided by your canning supplier.

To pickle MUSHROOMS brown.

Pickled Mushrooms

TAKE a quart of large mufhroom buttons, wafh them in allegar with a flannel, take three anchovies and chop them fmall, a few blades of mace, a little pepper and ginger, a fpoonful of falt, and three cloves of fhalots, put them into a faucepan with as much allegar as will half cover them, fet them on the fire, and let them ftew till they fhrink pretty much ; when cold put them in fmall bottles with the allegar poured upon them, cork and tie them up clofe. This pickle will make a great addition in brown fauce.

Mushroom buttons, as needed
3 anchovies
1 teaspoon ground mace
Pepper, as needed
Ginger, as needed
1 tablespoon salt
3 shallots

➢ For pickled mushrooms: Clean two pounds of mushrooms removing the stems. Using a stock pot, create a brine by combining two cups of distilled water, three-quarter cup of 5% white **VINEGAR**, one tablespoon of salt, three anchovies minced, three shallots sliced thin and separated, one teaspoon of ground mace, and one-half teaspoon each of ground ginger and crushed black peppercorn. Bring to a boil. Allow to cool to room temperature. Your mushrooms are ready to be canned using the brine. Follow the canning directions provided by your canning supplier.

For preserving Strawberries.

Strawberry Preserves

Take two quarts of Strawberries, squeeze them through a cloth, add half a pint of water and two pound of sugar, put it into a sauce pot, scald and skim it, take two pound of Strawberries with stems on, set your sauce pot on a chaffing dish, put as many Strawberries into the dish as you can with the stems up without bruising them, let them boil for about ten minutes, then take them out gently with a fork and put them into a stone pot for use; when you have done the whole turn the sirrup into the pot, when hot; set them in a cool place for use.

➢ For strawberry preserves: Clean and remove the stems from strawberries. Puree the strawberries using a food processor. Using a sauce pot, combine puree with two ounces of fruit pectin and six cups of granulated sugar for every three pounds of puree. Place whole strawberries sliced in half into sanitized canning jars. Boil the puree, stirring to prevent burning, until the temperature reaches 220°F [test the temperature of the puree with a candy thermometer]. Remove from heat and pour into the canning jars with the strawberries. Cover the jars with lids and allow to cool. Alternate method: Add one tablespoon lemon juice to the puree.

To preserve Peaches.

Peach Preserves

Put your peaches in boiling water, just give them a scald, but don't let them boil, take them out, and put them in cold water, then dry them in a sieve, and put them in long wide mouthed bottles: to half a dozen peaches take a quarter of a pound of sugar, clarify it, pour it over your peaches, and fill the bottles with brandy, stop them close, and keep them in a close place.

> ➢ For peach preserves: Peel and remove the seed from ripe peaches. Puree the peaches using a food processor. Using a sauce pot, combine puree with two ounces of fruit pectin and six cups of granulated sugar for every three pounds of puree. Slice whole peaches into eight pieces putting them into sanitized canning jars. Boil the puree, stirring to prevent burning, until the temperature reaches 220°F [test the temperature of the puree with a candy thermometer]. Remove from heat, quickly whisking in two tablespoons of **BRANDY** for every pound of puree and pour into the canning jars with the sliced peaches. Cover the jars with lids and allow to cool.

Jams, Jellies and Marmalades

Apricot jam.

Apricot Jam

HAVING procured fome of the ripeft; apricots, pare and cut them thin. Then infufe them in an earthen pan till they be tender and dry. To every pound and a half of apricots, put a pound of double refined fugar, and three fpoonfuls of water. Boil your fugar to a candy height, and then put it upon your apricots. Stir them over a flow fire till they look clear and thick ; but obferve, that they must only fimmer, and not boil. You may then put them into your glaffes.

- For apricot jam: Peel and remove the seed from ripe apricots. Puree the apricots using a food processor. Using a sauce pot, combine the puree with two ounces of fruit pectin, one cup of water and two cups of granulated sugar for every three pounds of apricots. Boil the puree, stirring to prevent burning, until the temperature reaches 220°F [test the temperature of the puree with a candy thermometer]. Remove from heat and immediately pour into sanitized canning jars covering with lids and allowing to cool.

- Alternate method: For every three pounds of puree, add one tablespoon of lemon juice.

Strawberry jam.

Strawberry Jam

BRUISE very fine fome fcarlet ftrawberries gathered when they be very ripe, and put to them a little juice of ftrawberries. Beat and lift their weight in fugar, ftrew it among them, and put them into the preferving-pan. Set them over a clear flow fire, fkim them, and boil them twenty minutes, and then put them into glaffes.

- For strawberry jam: Clean and remove the stems from strawberries. Puree the strawberries using a food processor. Using a sauce pot, combine the strawberry puree with two ounces of fruit pectin, one cup of water and two cups of granulated sugar for every three pounds of strawberries. Boil the puree, stirring to prevent burning, until the temperature reaches 220°F [test the temperature of the puree with a candy thermometer]. Remove from heat and immediately pour into sanitized canning jars covering with lids and allowing to cool.

- Alternate method: For every three pounds of puree, add one tablespoon of lemon juice.

Fruit in jelly.

Jell-O®

TAKE a bafon, put into it half a pint of clear ftiff calf's feet jelly, and when it be fet and ftiff', lay lay in three fine ripe peaches, and a bunch of grapes with the ftalk upwards. Put over them a few vine leaves, and then fill up your bowl with jelly. Let it ftand till the next day, and then fet your bafon to the brim in hot water. As foon as you perceive it gives way from the bafon, lay your difh over it, and turn your jelly carefully upon it. You may life flowers for your garnifh.

Boiling 10 pounds of bones should yield approximately four cups of gelatin; however, the amount of time required to retrieve the gelatin is time consuming. To simplify the process, the recipe will use unflavored gelatin.

- ➢ Follow the manufacturer's directions and prepare unflavored gelatin. Pour the gelatin into a mold with sliced ripe peaches and fresh grapes.

- ➢ Alternate method: Replace the water in the manufacture's gelatin recipe with juice [orange, grape, etc.].

The simplicity of this recipe allows for a variety of fruits to be used at the creator's discretion.

Orange Marmalade.

Orange Marmalade

CUT in two the cleareft Seville oranges you can get, take out all the pulp and juice into a bafon, and pick all the fkins and feeds out of it. Boil the rinds in hard water till they be tender, and change the water two or three times while they be boiling. Then pound them in a marble mortar, and add to it the juice and pulp. Then put them in the preferving pan with double its weight of loaf fugar, and fet it over a flow fire. Boil it rather more than half an hour, put it into pots, cover it with brandy paper, and tie it clofe down.

> For orange marmalade: Grate the peel and juice three pounds of oranges. Using a sauce pot, combine the orange juice and grated peel. For every one cup of orange juice, add one cup of granulated sugar with two ounces of fruit pectin. Bring to a boil. Continue to boil, stirring to prevent burning, until the temperature reaches 220°F [test the temperature of the juice with a candy thermometer]. Remove from heat and immediately pour into sanitized canning jars covering with lids and allowing to cool.

Apricot Marmalade,

Apricot Marmalade

ALL thofe apricots that are not good enough for preferves, or are too ripe for keeping, will anfwer this purpofe. Boil them in fyrup till they will mafh,

and then beat them in a marble mortar to a pafte. Take half their weight of loaf fugar, and put juft water enough to it to diffolve it. Boil and fkim it till it looks clear, and the fyrup thick like a fine jelly. Then put it into your fweet meat glaffes, and tie it up clofe.

> For apricot marmalade: Slice and remove the seed from ripe apricots. Puree apricots using a food processor. Using a sauce pot, combine the puree with two ounces of fruit pectin, one cup of water and two cups of granulated sugar for every three pounds of apricots. Boil, stirring to prevent burning, until the temperature reaches 220°F [test the temperature of the juice with a candy thermometer]. Remove from heat and immediately pour into sanitized canning jars covering with lids and allow to cool.

Candies

Rafpberry pafte.
Raspberry Candy

After you have wafh'd the rafpberries, drain half of them; and put the juice to the other half with the feeds ; fet them on the fire, and boil them apace for a quarter of an hour, and put half a pint of red currants boil'd with a very little water for a quarter of an hour, and drained through a thin strainer, to a pint of rafpberries; boil both rafpberries and currants together a little while ; then to a quart of juice put two pound and a half of fifted fugar; fet it over the fire, let it fcald, but not boil; pour it into little pots, fet it in the ftove till it is candied, then turn it on glaffes as other cakes.

> Raspberry, as needed
> Currants, as needed
> Sugar, as needed

The key to this recipe is "fet it in the stove till it is candied". By placing the "little pots" in the stove, the temperature of the sugar will increase creating the hard candy.

> ➢ For raspberry candy: Puree one-half pound each of raspberries and red currants [substitute red cherries]. Strain through a fine sieve. Using a sauce pot, combine the puree, one and one-half pounds of granulated sugar, and one-quarter cup

201

of water to every cup of puree. Bring to a boil and allow to boil, stirring to prevent the sugar from burning, until the temperature reaches 308°F [test the temperature of the puree with a candy thermometer]. Remove from heat and pour into candy molds and allow to cool.

- Alternate method: Use blackberries or blueberries instead of raspberries.
- Alternate method: Add one-quarter cup of lemon juice to the pureed fruit.

Burnt almonds.
French Praline

PUT two pounds of almonds, the fame quantity of loaf fugar, and a pint of water, into a ftew-pan. Set them over a clear coal fire, and let them boil till you hear the almonds crack. Then take them off, and ftir them about till they be quite dry. Put them in a wire fieve, and lift all the fugar from them. Put the fugar into the pan again with a little water, and give it a boil. Then put four fpoonfuls of fcraped cochineal to the fugar to colour it, put the almonds into the pan, and keep ftirring them over the fire till they be quite dry. Then put them into a glafs, and they will keep a year.

2 pounds almonds
2 pounds granulated sugar
Water, as needed
Cochineal, as needed

➢ For French pralines: Using a sauce pot, combine two pounds each of almonds and granulated sugar, and one cup of water. Bring to a boil and begin stirring the almonds. Keep stirring the almonds until all the water has evaporated and the almonds are dry. Reduce the temperature to medium and stir in eight ounces of granulated sugar. Keep stirring until all the sugar has melted coating the almonds and the color of the sugar is medium dark brown. Spread them out onto a baker's sheet pan lined with parchment paper keeping them apart so they do not stick together.

Lemon and Orange Peels candied.
Candied Peels

TAKE either lemons or oranges, cut them longways, take out all the pulp, and put the rinds into a pretty strong falt and hard water for fix days. Then boil them in a large quantity of fpring-water till they be tender. Take them out, and lay them on a hair fieve to drain. Then make a thin fyrup of fine loaf fugar, a pound to a quart of water. Put in your peels, and boil them half an hour, or till they look clear, and have ready a thick fyrup, made of fine loaf fugar, with as much water as will diffolve it. Put in your peels, and boil them over a flow fire till you fee the fyrup candy about the pan and peels. Then take them out, and grate fine fugar all over them. Lay them on a hair fieve to drain, and fet them in a ftove, or before the fire, to

dry. Remember when you boil either lemons or oranges, not to cover your faucepan.

> Lemon or Orange rind, cut into thin strips
> Salt, as needed
> Water, as needed

➤ For candied lemon or orange peel: Peel the fruit cutting off the white pith. Cut each peel into strips placing the peels into a sauce pot and add enough water to cover the peels. Bring to a boil. Reduce the temperature to medium-low allowing to simmer until the peels are soft. Drain the peels and return them to the pot. Place one-half cup each of granulated sugar and water in a second sauce pot and simmer until the sugar is dissolved. Add enough syrup to the peels to cover them. Bring to a boil and continue to boil, stirring to prevent the sugar from burning, until the temperature reaches 220°F [use a candy thermometer]. Drain the candy peels and evenly coat with granulated sugar.

Wines

Blackberry Wine.

Blackberry Wine

HAVING procured berries that are full ripe, put them into a large veffel of wood or ftone, with a cock in it, and pour upon them as much boiling water as will cover them. As foon as the heat will permit you to put your hand into the veffel, bruife them well till all the berries be broken. Then let them ftand covered till the berries begin to rife towards the top, which they ufually do in three or four days. Then draw off the clear into another veffel, and add to every ten quarts of this liquor one pound of fugar. Stir it well in, and let it ftand to work, a week or ten days, in another veffel like the firft. Then draw it off at the cock through a jellybag into a large veffel. Take four ounces of ifinglalf, and lay it to fteep twelve hours in a pint of white wine. The next morning, boil it upon a ftow fire till it be all diffolved. Then take a gallon of your blackberry juice, put in the diffolved ifinglafs, give them a boil together, and pour all into the veffel. Let it ftand a few days to purge and fettle, then draw it off, and keep it in a cool place.

Cherry Wine.

WHEN your cherries be full ripe, pull them off the ftalks, and prefs them through a hair fieve. To every gallon of liquor put two pounds of lump-fugar finely beaten, then ftir it together, and put it into a veffel, which mun: be filled. When it has done working, and ceafes to make any noife, ftop it clofe for three months, and bottle it off.

Orange Wine.

TAKE twelve Pounds of the beft Powder-fugar, with the Whites of eight or ten Eggs well beaten, into fix Gallons of Spring-water, and boil it three quarters of an Hour. When it is cold, put it into fix Spoonfuls of Yeaft, and alfo the Juice of twelve Lemons, which being pared muftftand with two Pounds of white Sugar in a Tankard, and in the Morning skim off the Top, and then put it into the Water. Then add the Juice and Rinds of fifty Oranges, but not the white Part of the Rinds; and fo let it work all together two Days and two Nights ; then add two Quarts of Rhenifh or White Wine, and put it into your Veffel.

Grape Wine.

White or Red Wine

TO a gallon of grapes put a gallon of water. Bruife the grapes, let them ftand a week without ftirring, and then draw it off fine. Put to a gallon of the wine three pounds of fugar, and then put it into a veffel, but do not flop it till it has done hiffing.

The discussion of Wine

Fruits ripened on the vine collect natural yeast on the skin. When the fruit is crushed or pressed, the natural yeast dissolves into the fruit juice; however, when juicing oranges, the natural yeast is discarded with the rind.

During the 18TH century, wines still had active yeast in the bottle. Adding white wine to fresh squeezed juice started the natural fermentation process. Today's wine has an ingredient added to kill the active yeast and stop fermentation or the wine is pasteurized. Because modern wine does not contain active yeast, the instruction in the recipe for adding wine is ignored.

When making orange wine, the recipe calls for the use of egg whites. Egg whites are used to clarify the juice removing any pulp.

You cannot use store purchased juices because they too have an ingredient to stop fermentation and it will kill any live active yeast added to the juice or they have been pasteurized.

> Using a vegetable/fruit juice extractor, collect one gallon of juice. Using a large stock pot, combine the juice with 32 ounces of granulated sugar. Heat using medium temperature, stirring occasionally, until the sugar has dissolved. Remove from heat and allow to cool to room temperature. Stir one package of brewer's yeast [5g, .176oz, one and one-quarter teaspoon] nutrient [follow manufacturer's directions for the nutrient] into the juice. Cover the pot with cheese cloth and allow to rest in a cool area. The juice will foam. Once the foam has settled, pour [racking] into a two-gallon carboy [jug] and stop with a brewer's airlock. You must use an airlock to prevent any oxygen from entering the bottle or the result will be vinegar. Allow to rest in a cool place for the next 14 days. After 14 days, pour off the juice [racking] leaving any sediment at the bottom of the carboy. Clean and sanitize the carboy and return the juice to the carboy. Stop the carboy with a brewer's airlock. Allow to rest for seven days. After seven days, pour off the juice [racking] a second time leaving any sediment at the bottom of the carboy. Clean and sanitize the carboy and return the juice to the carboy. Stop the carboy with a brewer's airlock. Allow to rest for seven days. After seven days, using a stock pot, heat the wine, stirring regularly, to 155°F. Remove from heat and rapidly cool. The wine is ready for bottling and aging. Follow the manufacturer's directions when adding potassium sorbate to

stop any further fermentation.

- For every gallon of finished orange, cherry, or blackberry wine, add one-quarter cup of lemon juice.

- If the finished wine is dry, add simple syrup one-quarter cup at a time to taste. For simple syrup, dissolve one cup of granulated sugar in one cup of hot water and allow to cool.

Note: Raspberry or blackberry juice is made with equal amounts of fruit puree and water or 16 ounces of fruit puree and 16 ounces of non-chlorinated water.

Fortified Wine

Combine four parts of wine to one part of brandy. Example: To make Marsala, combine 16 ounces of white wine with four ounces of brandy.

Fortified Wines

To Make	Combine with Brandy
Marsala	White Wine
Vermouth	White Wine flavored with herbs and spices
Sherry	Palomino, Muscat, or Pedro Ximeneze Grape Wine
Port	Fortified

Common herbs used in making Vermouth are: Thyme, basil, sage, rosemary, orange peel, vanilla, and oregano.

Ciders, Beer and Ale

Cider.

Cider

> Using a vegetable/fruit juice extractor, collect one gallon of juice. Using a stock pot, combine the juice with 32 ounces of granulated sugar. Heat using medium temperature, stirring occasionally, until sugar has dissolved. Allow to cool to room temperature. When cool, add one package of brewer's yeast [5g, .176oz, or one and one-quarter teaspoon] with yeast nutrient [follow manufacturer's directions for the nutrient] to the juice. Cover the pot with cheese cloth and allow to rest in a cool area. The juice will foam. Once the foam has settled, pour [racking] into a two-gallon carboy [jug] and stop with a brewer's airlock. You must use an airlock to prevent any oxygen from entering the bottle or the result will be vinegar. Allow the juice to ferment in a cool place for the next 14 days. After 14 days, pour off the juice [racking] leaving any sediment at the bottom of the carboy. Clean and sanitize the carboy and return the juice to the carboy. Stop the carboy with a brewer's airlock. Allow to rest for seven days. After seven days, pour off the juice [racking] leaving any sediment at the bottom of the carboy. Clean and sanitize the carboy and return the juice to the carboy. Stop the carboy with a brewer's airlock. Allow to rest for seven days. After seven days, using a stock pot, heat

the wine, stirring regularly, to 150°F. Remove from heat and rapidly cool. The wine is ready for bottling and aging. Follow the manufacturer's directions when adding potassium sorbate to stop any further fermentation.

- Alternate method: Combine 96 ounces of apple juice with 32 ounces of juice from raspberries, blackberries, or peaches.

Note: Raspberry or blackberry juice is made with equal amounts of fruit and water or 16 ounces of fruit puree to 16 ounces of non-chlorinated water.

For brewing Spruce Beer.

Spruce Beer

Take four ounces of hops, let them boil half an hour in one gallon of water, strain the hop water then add sixteen gallons of warm water, two gallons of molasses, eight ounces of essence of spruce, dissolved in one quart of water, put it in a clean cask, then shake it well together, add half a pint of emptins, then let it stand and work one week, if very warm weather less time will do, when it is drawn off to bottle, add one spoonful of molasses to every bottle.

4 ounces hops
Water, as needed
2 gallons molasses

8 ounces essence of spruce
8 ounces emptins

> For spruce beer: Using a stock pot, combine eight ounces of non-chlorinated water and one-quarter ounce of hops. Bring to a boil. Reduce the temperature to medium-low allowing to simmer for 30 minutes. Strain the hops reserving the water. Combine the reserved water with one gallon of warm non-chlorinated water. Stir two tablespoons essence of spruce into two tablespoons of non-chlorinated water. Stir 32 ounces of molasses and essence of spruce into the warm gallon of water. Continue to stir until molasses has dissolved. Allow to cool to room temperature. Stir one package of brewer's yeast [5g, .176oz, or one and one-quarter teaspoon] into the water. Allow to rest for seven days. Bottle the beer using 12-ounce bottles. Spoon one teaspoon of molasses into each bottle filled.

Emptins.

Leavening

Take a handful of hops and about three quarts of water, let it boil about fifteen minutes, then make a thickening as you do for starch, strain the liquor, when cold put a little emptins to work them, they will keep well cork'd in a bottle five or six weeks.

Substitute: Whisk together one cup of bread flour,

two cups of warm water, and one-quarter teaspoon active dry yeast. Place in an airtight jar. Once per day, open the jar and stir the flour. After one week, the emptins will be ready for use.

Cordials and Waters

Lemon Brandy.

Lemon Brandy

PUT five quarts of water to one gallon of brandy, take two dozen of lemons, two pounds of the beft fugar, and three pints of milk. Pare the lemons very thin, and lay the peel to fteep in the brandy twelve hours. Squeeze the lemons upon the fugar, then put the water to it, and mix all the ingredients together. Boil the milk, and pour it in boiling hot. Let it Hand twenty-four hours, and then ftrain it.

Orange Brandy.

Orange Brandy

PUT the chips of eighteen Seville oranges into three quarts of brandy, and let them fteep a fortnight in a done bottle clofe ftopped. Boil two quarts of fpring-water with a pound and a half of the fineft fugar, near an hour very gently. Clarify the water and fugar with the white of an egg, then ftrain it through a jelly bag, and boil it near half away. When it is cold, ftrain the brandy into the fyrup.

Rafpberry Brandy.

Raspberry Brandy

TAKE a pint of water and two quarts of brandy, and put them into a pitcher large enough to hold them and four pints of rafpberries. Put in half a pound of loaf fugar, and let it remain for a week clofe covered. Then take a piece of flannel, with a piece of Holland over it, and let it run through by degrees. It may be racked into other bottles a week after, and then it will be perfectly fine.

1/4 cup water
1/4 cup sugar
2 cups brandy
2 cups fruit puree

- Brandy is a byproduct of distilling wine and aging in wooden casks or barrels.

- For raspberry or blackberry brandy, puree the fruit adding it to the brandy.

- For lemon or orange brandy, juice four large lemons or two large oranges adding the juice and peel to the brandy.

> For infused brandy: Using a two-quart canning jar, combine two cups of brandy with the fruit puree, lemons, or oranges. Place a lid on the jar and shake. Let stand for 30 days. Strain the brandy using a fine wire sieve. Using a sauce pot, combine one-quarter cup each of water and granulated

sugar. Heat over medium temperature, stirring occasionally, until the sugar has dissolved. Allow the syrup to cool to room temperature. Combine with the infused brandy and bottle.

> Combine one-part brandy with two parts ginger ale. Serve on the rocks.

Peppermint water.
Mint Water

YOUR peppermint muft be gathered when it be full grown, and before it feeds. Cut it in fhort lengths, fill your ftill with it, and cover it with water. Then make a good fire under it, and when it be near boiling, and the ftill begins to drop, if your fire be too hot, draw a little from under it, as you fee occafion, to keep it from boiling over, or your water will be muddy. The flower your ftill drops, the clearer and ftronger will be your water ; but do not fpend it too far. The next day bottle it, and let it ftand three or four days, to take off the fiery tafte of the ftill. Then cork it well, and it will keep a long time.

Peppermint leaf, as needed
Water, as needed

> For peppermint water: Using a sauce pot, combine four cups mint leaves [rubbing the

leaves between your hands to bruise them] with four cups of distilled water. Bring to a boil. Reduce the temperature to low. Allow to simmer for 60 minutes. Strain through a coffee filter, bottle, and refrigerate.

- Alternate method: For every one cup of distilled water, add two teaspoons of peppermint extract.

Rofe Water.

Rose Water

GATHER your red rofes when they be dry and full blown; pick off the leaves, and to every peck, put a quart of water. Then put them into a cold ftill, and make a flow fire under it ; for the flower you diftil it, the better it will be. Then bottle it, and in two or three days time you may cork it.

Two gallons dried rose flowers
1 quart water

- For rose water: Using a sauce pot, combine four cups dried centifolia rose pedals and four cups of distilled water. Bring to a boil. Reduce the temperature to low. Allow to simmer for 60 minutes. Strain through a coffee filter, bottle, and refrigerate.

Orange Water.

Orange Water

Diftil orange flowers with a gentle fire, in a glafs or earthen glaz'd alembick, adding the flower of lemons; take care to ftop it very clofe in a glafs bottle.

> Orange blossoms, as needed
> Lemon blossoms, as needed
> Water, as needed

- For orange water: Cut two Seville oranges into one-quarter inch slices. Slice a lemon into four quarters. Using a saucepot, combine one-quarter lemon, all the orange slices, and four cups of distilled water. Bring to a boil. Reduce the temperature to low. Allow to simmer for 60 minutes. Strain through a coffee filter, bottle, and refrigerate.

- Alternate method: For every one cup of distilled water, add two teaspoons of orange extract and one teaspoon of lemon extract. "

Sources

(n.d.). Retrieved from Digital files obtained from Archive Organization. : http://archive.org/

(n.d.). Retrieved from Digital files obtained from Candida Martinelli's Italophile Site. http://italophiles.com

(n.d.). Retrieved from Digital files obtained from Google Books. https://books.google.com/

(n.d.). Retrieved from Digital files obtained from Gutenberg Project. https://www.gutenberg.org/

(n.d.). Retrieved from Digital files obtained from Library of Congress. https://loc.gov/

(n.d.). Retrieved from https://medical-dictionary.thefreedictionary.com/Suppressed+immune+systems.

(n.d.)., M.-W. (2021, July 3). Broth. Retrieved from Merriam-Webster.com dictionary.: https://www.merriam-webster.com/dictionary/broth

1746 George II Silver Sixpence "LIMA". (2021, July 9). Retrieved from BullionByPost: https://www.bullionbypost.co.uk/collectible-coins/sixpence/1746-george-ii-silver-sixpence-lima/

A Comprehensive Hisotry Of Soy. (2021). Retrieved 6 10, 2021, from SoyInfo Center: https://www.soyinfocenter.com/HSS/history.php

au gratin. (2021, July 7). Retrieved from Merriam-Webster: https://www.merriam-webster.com/dictionary/au%20gratin

Bailey, N. (1736). Diffionarium Domejlicum. London: Printed for C. Hitch at the Red Lion, and C. Davis, both in Pater-Nofter-Row; and S. Austen at the Angel and Bible, In St. Paul's Church Yard.

Bean. (2021, July 18). Retrieved from New World Encyclopedia: https://www.newworldencyclopedia.org/entry/Bean#:~:text=%20New%20World%20beans%20%201%20Common%20beans.,the%20scarlet%20runner%20bean%20since%20most...%20More%20

Bell, R. (2016, May 25). Pastrami Returns to Its Russian Roots. Retrieved from National Geographic: https://www.nationalgeographic.com/culture/article/pastrami-comes-back-to-its-roots-in-russia

Bisque. (2021, July 3). Retrieved from Merriam-Webster: https://www.merriam-webster.com/dictionary/bisque

Bradley, R. (1732). Country Houfewife. London: Printed for D. Browne, at the Black-Swan without Temple-Bar, and T. Woodman, in Ruffel-ftreet, Covent-Garden.

Bramen, L. (2011, November 18). Cooking Through the Ages: A Timeline of Oven Invention. Retrieved from Smithsonian Magazine: https://www.smithsonianmag.com/arts-culture/cooking-through-the-ages-a-timeline-of-oven-inventions-380050/

Britannica, T. E. (2013, August 20). Weights and Measures. Retrieved from Encyclopedia Britannica: https://www.britannica.com/science/measurement-system/The-English-and-United-States-Customary-systems-of-weights-and-measures

Britannica, T. E. (2021, January 24). Stove. Retrieved from Encyclopedia Britannica: https://www.britannica.com/technology/stove

British coin specifications. (© Copyright 2021 Jewellery Quarter Bullion Ltd.). Retrieved from BullionByPost: https://www.bullionbypost.co.uk/info/british-coin-specifications/#:~:text=The%20coin%20was%20approximately%2012mm%20in%20diameter%20and,-%20King%20William%20IV%20and%20later%20Queen%-20Victoria.

Cabbage Flowers for Food. (2021, July 22). Retrieved from Aggie Horticulture: https://aggie-horticulture.tamu.edu/archives/parsons/publications/vegetabletravelers/broccoli.html

Casserole. (2021, July 7). Retrieved from Merriam-Webster: https://www.merriam-webster.com/dictionary/casserole

Cheese History. (© 2021 - History of Cheese). Retrieved 3 4, 2021, from History of Cheese: http://www.historyofcheese.com/cheese-history-section/

DAUPHINOISE POTATOES RECIPE. (2021, July 7). Retrieved from Philos Kitchen: https://philosokitchen.com/dauphinoise-potatoes-au-gratin/

Deviled Eggs History: From Rome To Your Home. (2018, November 2). Retrieved from North Carolina Egg Association: https://ncegg.org/deviled-eggs-history-from-rome-to-your-home/

DRAKE, J. (1991, May 30). History Is Full of Fava Beans. Retrieved from Los Angeles Times: https://www.latimes.com/archives/la-xpm-1991-05-30-fo-3453-story.html

Edgar, G. (2018, 12 28). A Brief History of Cheddar Cheese. Retrieved 3 3, 2021, from Saveur: https://www.saveur.com/history-of-cheddar-cheese/

Facts About Sixpence Coins. (2021, July 9). Retrieved from Silver Sixpence: https://silversixpence.com/facts-about-sixpence-coins/

Farley, J. (1787). The London Art of Cookery. London: Printed for J. S CATC HERD and J. V/ H I T A K E R, N« 12, B. LAW, N® 13, Ave-Maria-Lane ; and G. and T. WILKIE, .St. Paul's Church-Yard.

Fergusson, E. (1934). Mexican Cookbook. Santa Fe, New Mexico: The Rydal Press.

French Beans. (2021, July 18). Retrieved from Specialty Produce: https://www.specialtyproduce.com/produce/French_Beans_601.php#:~:text=French%20beans%27%20ancestors%20are%20native%20to%20South%20and,beans%20were%20introduced%20to%20France%20via%20the%20Conquistadors.

Frijoles Refritos. (2013, May 9). Retrieved from Eden Foods: https://www.edenfoods.com/articles/view.php?articles_id=320&rtn=1

Fritada: Pork, Beef or Venison Blood Stew. (2021, March 24). Retrieved from Guampedia: https://www.guampedia.com/fritada-pork-beef-or-venison-blood-stew/

Glasse, H. (1747). The Art of Cookery. London: Printed for the Author; and sold at Mrs. Ashburn's, a China-Shop, the Corner of Fleet-Ditch.

Glasse, H. (1775). The Art of Cookery. London: Printed for a Company of BookFellers.

gravy. (2021, June 19). Retrieved from Merriam-Webster: https://www.merriam-webster.com/dictionary/gravy#h1

gravy. (Copyright ©2021 by HarperCollins Publishers.). Retrieved from Collins: https://www.collinsdictionary.com/dictionary/english-french/gravy

Here Is The Definitive History Of Mankind's Finest Food: The Salad. (2017, December 6). Retrieved from HuffPost: https://www.huffpost.com/entry/evolution-of-the-salad_n_7101632

Herzog, D. J. (2020, April 20). How To Make Your Own Penicillin From Oranges. Retrieved from SURVIVOPEDIA: https://www.survivopedia.com/how-to-make-your-own-penicillin-from-oranges/

History of Cabbage - Where does Cabbage come from? (2021, July 22). Retrieved from Vegetable Facts: http://www.vegetablefacts.net/vegetable-history/history-of-cabbage/

History of Carrots. (2021, July 22). Retrieved from Vegetable Facts: http://www.vegetablefacts.net/vegetable-history/history-of-carrots/

History of Cider. (2021, July 11). Retrieved from Washington State University: https://cider.wsu.edu/history-of-cider/

HISTORY OF PEARS. (2021, July 22). Retrieved from USA Pears: https://usapears.org/history-of-pears/

History of Potatoes. (2021, July 22). Retrieved from Vegetable Facts: http://www.vegetablefacts.net/vegetable-history/history-of-potatoes/

How To Make Blue Cheese Cultures. (Copyright © 2021 Curd Nerd). Retrieved from Curd Nerd: https://curd-nerd.com/cultivate-your-own-blue-mold/

Innocentis, I. D. (2020, November 13). The History Of Broccoli: From The Etruscan Period To Now. Retrieved from La Cucina Italiana: https://www.lacucinaitaliana.com/trends/healthy-food/history-broccoli-etruscans-today?refresh_ce=

Kelly, J. (2021). How Fireplaces Work. Retrieved from howstuff wo?ks: https://home.howstuffworks.com

Lake E. High, J. S. (2021, July 27). A Very Brief History of the Four Types of Barbeque Found In the USA. Retrieved from South Carolina Barbeque Association: https://web.archive.org/web/20170313171657/https://www.scbarbeque.com/index.php/2014-01-26-09-56-40

Lea, A. (1997, 2015). Part 3 - Juicing and Fermenting. Retrieved from THE SCIENCE OF CIDERMAKING: http://www.cider.org.uk/part3.htm#:

M.D., I. N. (1937, April 23). The mechanism of milk clotting. Retrieved from American Journal of Digestive Diseases and Nutrition: https://doi.org/10.1007/BF02999972

Martino, M. (between 1460 and 1480). Libro de arte coquinaria. Northern Italy.

May, R. (1685). The Accomplished Cook. London: Printed for Obadiah Blagrave at the Bear and Star in St. Pauls Church-Yard,.

MAYER, L. (2008, November 26). A Brief History of Pie. Retrieved from TIME: https://time.com/3958057/history-of-pie/

McCord, G. (2013, 4 26). All About Roquefort Cheese. Retrieved 3 3, 2021, from KQED: https://www.kqed.org/bayareabites/59940/all-about-roquefort-cheese

O'Neil, D. (2011, February 19). *How To Make Vermouth*. Retrieved from ART OF DRINK: https://www.artofdrink.com/ingredient/how-to-make-vermouth

Our Cheeses. (© 2018 Dunlop Dairy). Retrieved 3 3, 2021, from Dunlop Dairy: http://dunlopdairy.co.uk/cheese.html

Pease Porridge Hot. (Copyright © 2021 All Nursery Rhymes). Retrieved from All Nursery Rhymes: https://allnurseryrhymes.com/pease-porridge-hot/

Pegge, S. (1390). The Forme Of Cury. by the Master-Cooks of King RICHARD II, Presented afterwards to Queen ELIZABETH, by EDWARD Lord STAFFORD, And now in the Possession of GUSTAVUS BRANDER, Esq.: 2008 by Forgotten Books.

Product Reviews / Main Nibbles / Cookies The History of Biscotti. (2021, July 23). Retrieved from The Nibble: https://www.thenibble.com/reviews/main/cookies/cookies2/the-origin-of-biscotti.asp

QUICHE ORIGINS. (since 1999). Retrieved from FoodReference.com: http://www.foodreference.com/html/artquiche.html

Raffald, E. (1786). The Experienced Englisfh Housfekeeper. LONDON: PRINTED FOR R , BALDWIN.

Red Beans & Rice 101. (2021, July 18). Retrieved from Zatarain's: https://www.mccormick.com/zatarains/red-beans-and-rice#Origin

Rindskipf, J. (2021, June 15). Foods that are dangerous if not prepared properly. Retrieved from MSN powered by Microsoft News: https://www.msn.com/en-us/health/nutrition/foods-that-are-dangerous-if-not-prepared-properly/ss-AAL4YcE#image=1

Rupp, R. (2014, July 22). The History of the "Forbidden" Fruit. Retrieved from National Geographic: https://www.nationalgeographic.com/culture/article/history-of-apples

SANTONASTASO, T. (2020, May 29). A BRIEF HISTORY OF PASTA. Retrieved from italics Magazine: https://italicsmag.com/2020/05/29/a-brief-history-of-pasta/

Savoiardi Biscuits. (2016, January 18). Retrieved from Sicilian Cooking Plus: https://siciliancookingplus.com/recipe-items/savoiardi-biscuits/

scallop. (2021, July 7). Retrieved from Merriam-Webster: https://www.merriam-webster.com/dictionary/scalloped

Simmons, A. (1796). American Cookery. Hartford: PRINTED BY HUDSON & GOODWIN, FOR THE AUTHOR.

Smith, C. (2017, 10 5). The History of Cheesemaking. Retrieved 3 3, 2021, from The Chester Lecture Society: http://chesterlecturesociety.org/the-history-of-cheesemaking/

Smith, E. (1773). The Complete Housewife. London: Printed for J. Buckl.and, J. and F. Rivington, J. HintoNj Hawes, Clarke and Collins, W. Johnston, S. Crowder, T. Long MAN, B. Law, T. Lowndes, S. Be a don, W. Nicoll, and C. and R. Ware.

Smith, K. A. (2013, 6 18). Why the Tomato Was Feared in Europe for More Than 200 Years. Retrieved from Smithsonian Magazine: https://www.smithsonianmag.com/arts-culture/why-the-tomato-was-feared-in-europe-for-more-than-200-years-863735/

Soup. (2021, July 1). Retrieved from Merriam-Webster: https://www.merriam-webster.com/dictionary/soup

Spätzle. (Copyright © 2021 German Food Guide). Retrieved from German Food Guide.

Spinach History - Origins of Different Types of Spinach. (2021, July 22). Retrieved from Vegetable History: http://www.vegetablefacts.net/vegetable-history/spinach-history/

staff, M. (2020, November 8). Complete Guide to Fortified Wine: 6 Types of Fortified Wine. Retrieved from MasterClass: https://www.masterclass.com/articles/complete-guide-to-fortified-wine#:~:text=The%20basic%20process%20for%20making%20fortified%20wine%20involves,distilled%20spirits%20at%20different%-20stages%20of%20the%20process.

Standing, E. (2018, October 30). The English Origins of Sweet Potato Pie. Retrieved from Edmund Standing: https://edmundstanding.wordpress.com/2018/10/30/the-english-origins-of-sweet-potato-pie/

The English Fishery and Trade in the 18th Century. (2021, July 11). Retrieved from Newfoundland and Labrador Heritage: https://www.heritage.nf.ca/articles/exploration/18th-century-fishery.php

The Lady's Companion. (1753). London: Printed for J. HODGES, on London-Bridge; and R. BALDWIN, at the Rofe, in Peter-nofter Row.

The Origin of Cultivated Fruits and Vegetables. (© 2021 Arizona Board of Regents). Retrieved from Northern Arizona University: https://www2.nau.edu/lrm22/lessons/plant_origins/plant_origins.html

To 10 Cheeses. (© 2011 whatParis.com). Retrieved 3 4, 2021, from What Paris: https://www.whatparis.com/top-french-cheese.html

What is Pudding? (2011, November 15). Retrieved from British Food: A History: https://britishfoodhistory.com/2011/11/15/what-is-a-pudding/

White, C. (2010, August 31). How Pasteurization Works. Retrieved from howstuffworks.com: https://science.howstuffworks.com/life/cellular-microscopic/pasteurization.htm

www.ingramcontent.com/pod-product-compliance
Lightning Source LLC
LaVergne TN
LVHW010315070526
838199LV00065B/5564